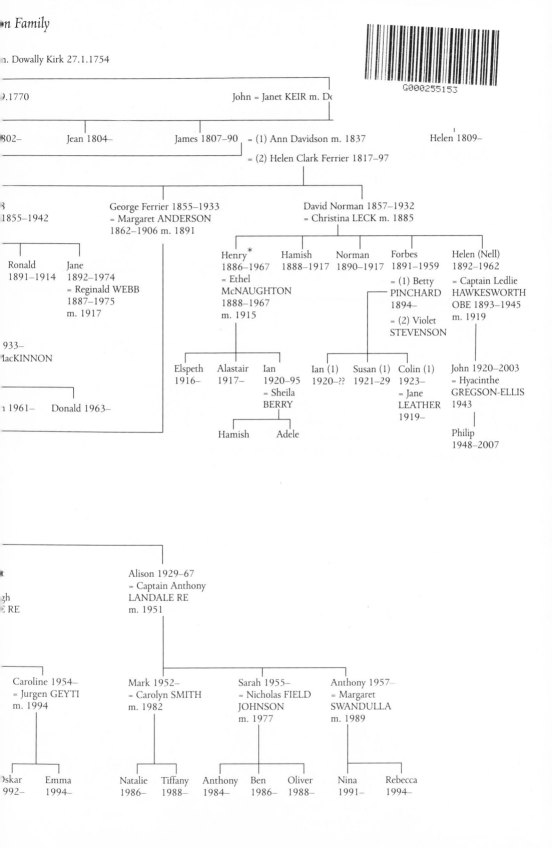

n. Dowally Kirk 27.1.1754

).1770   John = Janet KEIR m. D(

G000255153

802–   Jean 1804–   James 1807–90   = (1) Ann Davidson m. 1837   Helen 1809–

= (2) Helen Clark Ferrier 1817–97

8   George Ferrier 1855–1933   David Norman 1857–1932
1855–1942   = Margaret ANDERSON   = Christina LECK m. 1885
1862–1906 m. 1891

Ronald   Jane   Henry*   Hamish   Norman   Forbes   Helen (Nell)
1891–1914   1892–1974   1886–1967   1888–1917   1890–1917   1891–1959   1892–1962
= Reginald WEBB   = Ethel   = (1) Betty   = Captain Ledlie
1887–1975   McNAUGHTON   PINCHARD   HAWKESWORTH
m. 1917   1888–1967   1894–   OBE 1893–1945
m. 1915   = (2) Violet   m. 1919
STEVENSON

933–
MacKINNON

Elspeth   Alastair   Ian   Ian (1)   Susan (1)   Colin (1)   John 1920–2003
1916–   1917–   1920–95   1920–??   1921–29   1923–   = Hyacinthe
= Sheila   = Jane   GREGSON-ELLIS
1 1961–   Donald 1963–   BERRY   LEATHER   1943
1919–

Hamish   Adele   Philip
1948–2007

Alison 1929–67
= Captain Anthony
LANDALE RE
m. 1951

gh
E RE

Caroline 1954–   Mark 1952–   Sarah 1955–   Anthony 1957–
= Jurgen GEYTI   = Carolyn SMITH   = Nicholas FIELD   = Margaret
m. 1994   m. 1982   JOHNSON   SWANDULLA
m. 1977   m. 1989

)skar   Emma   Natalie   Tiffany   Anthony   Ben   Oliver   Nina   Rebecca
992–   1994–   1986–   1988–   1984–   1986–   1988–   1991–   1994–

HOMECOMING

HOMECOMING

A Memoir
Volume Three

Jill Ashley Miller

STRATHMORE PUBLISHING

LONDON

2010

First published in Great Britain by Strathmore Publishing,
41 Kingsway Place, Sans Walk, London ECIR 0LU, 2010

Designed and produced by David McLean (dhmcl7@gmail.com) in Manticore.
Illustrations from family sources originated by David McLean

Edited by Christopher Pick (christopher@the-picks.co.uk)

ISBN 978-0-9550887-8-0

Printed and bound by Portland Print, Kettering NN16 8UN

All the proceeds from this volume will be given to Norwich Mencap to create
an amenity fund for my Down's Syndrome daughter Catherine and her friends
George and Lennie. They moved in autumn 2008 to a 'Supported Living'
bungalow after living in their residential home, Burlingham House, for almost
thirty years. This fund will provide extras, for example plants for the garden
and taxis for trips to outside events such as Gateway clubs and the pantomime.

JAM

This book has been privately printed. Further copies may be obtained from
Mark Ashley Miller of The Present Finder Ltd, Unit 1, South Western Business
Park, Sherborne DT9 3PS (01935 815195) by letter or telephone; or from his
website, www.thepresentfinder.co.uk. All proceeds will be passed to Norwich
Mencap.

Frontispiece: My wedding day and in many ways also the day of my homecoming:
St Stephen's, Rochester Row, SW1, 11 February 1956.

Contents

The two loves of my life in their handsome youth: Lieutenant Commander Peter Ashley Miller in 1955; and Peter Dallas Ross in 1947.

To my two Peters,
Peter Ashley Miller, my husband, who gave me
forty-one years of happiness, and
Peter Dallas Ross, my first love, who returned
after fifty-three years to solace my widowhood.

Jilly on a chairlift at Hochsölden, Austria, in April 1955, taken by Peter.

Preface

And now I have reached the end. These three volumes of my memoirs have been absorbing to write, and I hope that they may be of interest to my descendants. All the quotations are from my diary which I kept religiously from 1941 to 1953: a pity that I stopped at that point just as my life was becoming more eventful.

My thanks, once again, to my brilliant designer, David McLean, and meticulous editor, Christopher Pick, without whom this would have been a poor thing. My thanks, too, to Caroline Irwin (the daughter of Angus and Elizabeth) for permission to reproduce her lovely portrait of Catherine on the back of the jacket, and also to those who sent me photographs: in particular, Peter Anson, who sent me five, and Mary Balfour, Miche's widow, who sent me one of him aged twenty-one. The remainder are from family sources.

The trees of both families, McNaughton and Kitson, skilfully compiled by David McLean, Christopher Pick and Talitha Minchin, appear on the endpapers of this book.

JILL ASHLEY MILLER
Beccles, September 2010

The marriage of my Wren friend Elizabeth Cumming to Captain Angus Irwin MC Black Watch at
St Michael's, Chester Square, 25 June 1946: the first of many such ceremonies I attended during the
post-war years.

Chapter 1

Adrift

'The sea will ebb and flow – heaven show his face'

Love's Labour's Lost 4.3.216

On 1 June 1946 I shed my Wren uniform and became a civilian.

The home in Englefield Green to which I returned was very different from the happy ménage of the war years. Gone were the smiling faces of Nancy and Sylvia, both now married,[1] and in their place was 'Mr Stewart', a cantankerous old man – at least I thought of him as 'old', though he was probably in his fifties. Nicotine-stained and garrulous, he liked to be called 'Binks', and was accompanied by a scruffy, smelly mongrel.

I knew that my mother needed to augment her small income with paying guests, and 'Binks' had arrived, I don't know from where, ostensibly to help with the gardening for a low rent. He and I disliked each other instantly. He was both untidy and incompetent. One day I arrived home, when my mother was away, to find he had flooded his bedroom, which used to be mine, and fused all the electricity by switching on an empty kettle. Although he was ex-Indian Army and outwardly respectable, I began to fear that, impressed with the cachet of lodging with an 'Hon.', he had an ulterior motive. We viewed each other warily.

Although the war was now over, there were still privations. One of my first tasks was to bike to Egham Food Office to register for a ration book. Sweets would remain rationed until 1953, and coupons were still required for clothes. Bread rationing was introduced this year, and many household groceries would not become available until 1948. Paper was in short supply and newspapers were limited to ten pages.

Meanwhile, men were coming back from the war.

My lifelong friend Jinny Lowe (*née* Wyllie) aged thirty-nine at home in Lower Halstow, Kent, in 1965.

Richard Vickers was the best-looking man I had ever seen: tall and dark with aquiline features. He would have had a certain future in Hollywood. With his twin brother Tom, who was equally handsome, he had come home to run Scaitcliffe, the renowned Eton prep school in Englefield Green started by his father in 1896. Unsurprisingly, the 'Vickers twins' were much in demand.

Early in June, Stella Brooke, Jinny Wyllie and I decided to celebrate the end of the war by throwing a party at the Savoy, then the most popular London hotel for the young. We gathered nine of our friends, and to our surprise Richard accepted. After an excellent dinner – 'scallops, duck and ice cream' – and dancing to Carroll Gibbons' band, we went on to the Astor night club. None of us was a member, so Jinny forged the name of a friend, Jean Ackroyd. Richard drove me home in the dawn and we said a chaste goodnight.

But forget romance – my most pressing need was to find a job. As I had only trained to be a secretary, the field was narrow. The parochial world of Englefield Green was becoming claustrophobic and the presence of 'Binks' at home a constant irritant. My sights were set on Oxford, where the magnet was 'Men'. No one suggested that I might get there academically, for ex-service people received generous grants if they had matriculated. But my lack of a Latin credit held me back.[2] Neither of my parents was academic, and my father's only suggestion was that I should become a press photographer. As I had no interest in photography, this was less than helpful.

I decided to write to the Bodleian. I did not analyse the

propulsion that pushed me towards books, for my father, now divorced and living in a dingy London bedsitter, had never talked of his family – indeed, he scarcely talked to me at all. I did not know that my forebears included eminent publishers, booksellers and novelists.[3] Soon, a letter arrived from Bodley's Librarian inviting me for an interview.

Small, dapper and in rimless pince-nez, Mr Harry Creswick was an academic with little to do. We chatted for over an hour. He asked about my family and whether I had a boyfriend, which I thought intrusive. He enquired whether I knew the meaning of the word 'provincial' and what it implied. He ended by telling me that he had never had a secretary and had only asked me to come because I had 'nice handwriting'. However, he thought that a colleague, the University Registrar, might have an opening. So I went to see Douglas Veale, who offered me a job at four pounds five shillings a week. Rooms in Oxford were hard to find, but I secured the option on one in Crick Road for three pounds ten shillings. Going home in the train, I did my arithmetic and realised that I would never manage on an income of fifteen shillings a week. Sadly, I wrote to refuse both offers. (Had I had more guts, I could have found a cheaper room, but my mother persuaded me that the whole idea was out of the question.)

On 25 June Liz Cumming, my old Wren friend, married Angus Irwin at St Michael's Chester Square; many ex-Wrens were there. The reception, at the Overseas League, a handsome eighteenth-century house overlooking Green Park, was the first I had attended where the toast was 'Your Majesty, Lords, Ladies and Gentlemen' – the exiled King George of Greece was an old friend of the Cummings and had spent much of the war with them. Angus' best man was Brigadier Bernard Fergusson.[4]

Early in July, with the shadow of Binks still hanging over me, Jinny and I set out on a long-hatched plan. The normal way to travel in wartime had been to hitch-hike, and the roads had been full of women in uniform thumbing a lift. Petrol was still in short supply (rationing did not end until 1950), and, as we could still wear our Wren uniform, this was how we intended to travel. Our mothers were anxious: 'Don't go anywhere near Bournemouth.' A vicious murder by a chap called Neville Heath had recently taken place there. We assured them that we would be very careful. There was a certain safety in uniform.

We set out from Jinny's home near Guildford and thumbed our way down the A3 towards Portsmouth. On the way we were treated to tea by 'a very nice Padre'. Our goal was to stay with my cousins, Harold and Hilly Wyllie, who had entertained me as a Wren in Southsea. They had moved from Gosport to Tower House, overlooking Portsmouth harbour, which Harold had inherited from his father, the celebrated marine artist W L Wyllie. Jinny was an instant success – she and Harold discovered they were third cousins and he liked 'the cut of her jib' so much that she was enjoined to stay whenever she liked. Harold was also an artist, though some people found his meticulous style inferior to the more romantic lines of his father. From his studio at the top of the house he could see the constant movement of shipping in the harbour, which inspired many of his best pictures. He showed us a watercolour his father had painted under water. He had experimented with various devices, and had succeeded by sitting in a water-tight contraption like a biscuit box with a glass front.

The next day, they took us sailing in their 20 foot 'Victory' class boat, *Sapristi*, my first experience of sailing

Our next stop was Weymouth, via Beaulieu in the New Forest. Unfortunately, with the insouciance of youth, we had failed to confirm our arrival to some friends of my mother, the Meeks, with whom we had arranged to stay. The house was locked and there was clearly no one at home. It was now growing dark and the hotels were full. The prospect of spending the night on the streets was not appealing. Fortunately the Wrennery had not yet been disbanded, and as we were in uniform a kindly Petty Officer took us in.

On to Devon, where Jinny had friends living on the edge of Dartmoor at Ivybridge. The Sparrows were a horsy family – pictures, table mats and silver all did homage to the horse. As I knew little about this animal, except for a bolting pony in Richmond Park when I was nine, I was somewhat out of my depth. However, we were soon put at ease by their daughter, Sally, a FANY (First Aid Nursing Yeomanry) who had just been demobbed.

The next hop was to Cornwall, where we had our only unpleasant experience. We were picked up by a lorry driver near Plymouth, and his suggestive remarks soon made it obvious that he had only one thing in mind. Fortunately, he stopped for a sandwich near Lostwithiel and we made our escape. We were lucky, and Jinny reminded me of her experience in Plymouth, some two years earlier, which might not have turned out so well. Wanting to get to a party some miles distant and wearing uniform, she had thumbed a lift from a spotty youth driving a white van. Having asked her destination, he drove some way on the main road, then, to her consternation, turned down a muddy track. Here he stopped beside a field. With mounting panic, she asked him what on earth he thought he was doing. 'Miss,' he replied, breathing heavily, 'Let me have a feel, please Miss.'

With crisp asperity, Jinny told him to drive on. Recognising in her voice generations of colonial authority, the young man obeyed. She had a lucky escape.

We were making for Falmouth, to the home of Jo Newham, a Wren friend of Jinny's. Her father and I did not take to each other – 'a most bombastic man', I noted in my diary. I was wearing Helena Rubinstein's newest shade of lipstick, Pink Champagne, to which he took exception, saying it was a ghastly colour. He asked me why all the people we were staying with were friends of Jinny. 'Where are your friends?' he enquired unpleasantly.

Then on to Westward Ho!, where my diary does not record with whom we stayed. We had now been away for a week. Although we had planned to have another two days, when I rang my mother that night she sounded so low that I knew I had to get home. 'You're all I've got' would become a constant mantra.

Next day we left at seven-thirty, and arrived at Barnstaple in half an hour. Then we went on by slow stages to Taunton which we reached by eleven o'clock. Here we had 'incredible luck'. A passing staff car picked us up and drove us the 150 miles to Sunningdale. I was home by five-thirty.

Jinny had been the perfect travelling companion – stimulating, amusing and relaxed. The short trip cemented our lifelong friendship. 'Jinny is as near a Saint as possible and I am feeling a better person for having been with her.'

Life in Englefield Green dragged on with my mother and I becoming increasingly irritable. She told me that I had grown hard and never helped with the housework. Among our neighbours was a delightful woman, Marjorie Armstrong, who took me under her wing. She made hats as a sideline and had a small boutique in Burlington Arcade. One day she asked me if I would like to go to the Eton and Harrow cricket match and made me a delicious little hat of pale blue petals to go with a new dress. Among the crowds at Lords, I found several of my Wren friends, one of whom, Pam Wilson, who lived in Perthshire, asked me to stay for 'The Twelfth', the start of the grouse-shooting season.

And so it was that on 8 August I found myself in the night sleeper heading north. All the berths had gone, so I sat up and arrived in Perth at five o'clock. After a bath and breakfast at the Station Hotel, I caught the local train to Blairgowrie, where Pam and her father met me. Ashmore, the Wilsons' estate, was near the small village of Bridge of Cally, and was surrounded by miles of moorland. Pam had invited two other friends, Anne Shuttleworth and Joy Bowyer, to stay, and that night we were fourteen for dinner. Although I had barely slept in the train, we danced eightsomes until two o'clock. Among the guests was an American General Bissell with his wife and daughter. There were also two young men, Peter Shaw in the Black Watch and Norman Fraser, a Cameron Highlander whom I describe as 'the nicest'. The next day the house was 'in a turmoil' as we all got ready for a huge fête in aid of prisoners of war. Marquees and tents covered the lawn – Pam, Joy, Anne and I were roped in to help with ices, drinks and shove ha'penny. That night three RAF chaps arrived. From a lofty height, my twenty-year-old self opined that they were 'awfully young, about nineteen'. They included Michael Barber, whom I describe as 'rather quiet and shy, but the most interesting', and Tony Caillard, enormous at 6 feet 5 inches, 'a little conceited, but charming', who later became an Air Vice-Marshal; and Frazer Sedcole, who went on to have a distinguished career in Unilever, Reed International and Tate and Lyle. After they left, Colonel (not Mrs) Wilson received a 'thank-you' letter from one of them beginning 'Dear Lieutenant-Colonel Wilson'. 'Good God!' he snorted, 'Where was the fella educated?' The day of the Twelfth was dull with light rain, but we trudged across the miles of heather and the guns secured a bag of 110 brace.

The return home was an anti-climax. The ubiquitous presence of 'Binks' grated as he began to take over the cottage. One day, I found his photograph standing prominently on the mantelpiece and was filled with foreboding My mother, always susceptible to male flattery, lapped up his attention and I dreaded the thought that he might become my new 'father'. I was told that I was 'off-hand' with him, and the situation was becoming impossible. Things came to a head when my mother issued an ultimatum saying that either he or I must go. My Oxford plans had come to nothing. It was time to move on.

Stella had just started dance training at a college in Holyport, a village near Maidenhead. The two Principals needed a residential secretary. Starved of young companionship after the Wrens, I decided to take the job. The pay was £3 a week, plus board and lodging, which seemed generous.

The London College of Dance had been founded by three Jewish sisters, the Misses Cone, known respectively as 'Miss Lily, Miss Gracie and Miss Valerie'. Originally from London, they had recently moved into a large house, 'The Lodge', which overlooked Holyport's village green. The house's main claim to fame was that it possessed one of the few real tennis courts in the country.

The comprehensive three-year course included ballet, tap, ballroom dancing and 'Natural Movement' as well as anatomy and physiology. The joint Principals were Miss Madge Atkinson, a small, dumpy grey-haired woman in her sixties, and Miss Anita Heyworth, about forty-two, whose graceful deportment and black hair swept into a bun suggested Spanish ancestry. As they shared a bedroom, there were the inevitable rumours, but they were more like mother and daughter. We heard later that the younger woman had been raped by her father which had, understandably, put her off men.

The first few weeks went well and my pleasure increased when Jinny decided to do the course. It was a tricky situation for me as I was firmly 'Staff', sitting at the staff table during meals, and was supposed to have little to do with the students. Gradually, the all-female establishment began to stultify, and I wished that I had stipulated a term's trial.

The end of the war saw the familiar pattern of life restored. Several of my friends came of age that year and were thinking about that rite of passage, their twenty-first parties. These dances were not only an excuse for jollification but also, more importantly, a marriage market. The only problem was the shortage of men. The carnage of the last six years meant that there were very few of these desirable creatures around, and it was obligatory, if asked to a party, to bring a partner, unless one wanted to spend the evening as a wallflower.

By October, plans for my own dance on 16 November were well under way. A friend of my mother, Frank Saunders, a rich business-man and Chairman of Court Shipping Line, generously offered his Queen Anne house in Englefield Green. He and his wife, Elsie, had no children and enjoyed the vicarious pleasure of entertaining their young friends. It was the custom for the dates of dances to be announced in the social column of *The Times*. Although Frank urged my mother to do this (naturally mentioning that the Hon. Mrs McNaughton was giving a dance for her daughter and that it was taking place at Dial House, Englefield Green by kind permission of Mr Frank Saunders), I was thankful that she resisted.

About this time, we heard that Peter Dallas Ross's engagement had been broken off and that he was once more in circulation.[5] An invitation was hurriedly despatched.

Dress fabrics were still in short supply, but I managed to find some pretty rosepink silk which Miss Tedder, the village dress-maker in Englefield Green, made up into a long evening dress with the fashionable 'Bertha' neckline (low cut with a double frill).

A week beforehand, the stress of it all brought my face out in spots, but Cyclax' 'Special Lotion', which I had continued to use ever since I had been given free samples at Queen Charlotte's Ball in 1943,[6] soon removed them.

A few days before the dance, something happened that stirred all my latent memories of my sister Peggy, killed so tragically only six years earlier.[7] I was biking to Miss Tedder to collect my dress, without realising that Kipling, our wire-haired fox terrier, had followed me. A screech of brakes made me turn my head. There in the road was his limp body, blood pouring from his nose. A military car carrying a colonel had not seen him. He was barely alive and I thought there was no hope. I closed my eyes and saw once more the small shape of my sister beneath the wheels of the Devon General bus. The Colonel was very concerned and insisted on taking Kipling to the nearest vet. Happily he was merely shocked and there were no broken bones. If only, if only I could have said the same in 1940. The pain of her death would never leave me.

The days before the dance were spent in frantic preparation. Of all the men we had asked, there was only one whom I really wanted. When the telephone rang and a familiar voice said 'This is Peter Dallas Ross,' my heart leaped. He said that he was 'devastated' not to be able to come, but that his work as a plastic surgeon in the Birmingham Accident Hospital treating badly burned children meant that he could not get away. Sadly, I wrote in my diary. 'If Peter were coming, my cup would be running over.'

A page from my diary, 27 October 1945, with my reactions to the news of Peter Dallas Ross' engagement (see *Not the Purser's Daughter?*, page 130). 'Oh!, what hell it was when I saw this in The Times last Wednesday. I simply couldn't believe my eyes and felt quite stunned for a time....'

19

Orchard Cottage, Englefield Green, with Kipling on guard in the doorway.

On the evening of Friday 15 November, tiny Orchard Cottage, despite its three bedrooms, was crammed to the gunwales. I cannot imagine how we squeezed everyone in, but we managed to include, besides my mother and me, three cousins, Joyce, Beryl and Margaret, as well as my grandparents' butler and cook, Mr and Mrs Hemsley. The Hemsleys, although now pensioned off in their own Yorkshire cottage, were still very much part of our family and were included whenever possible. Hemsley had started his service with my grandfather as an under-footman, and was subsequently promoted to butler, in which position he spent the rest of his working life. He travelled everywhere with his employers, to Scotland, the Riviera and Australia. He had had the good sense to marry the kitchen-maid, who then became an excellent cook. And now, for my dance, although long retired, Mrs Hemsley had generously agreed to do 'the eats'.

I spent the evening opening my many presents. There was a pigskin handbag from cousins, a lighter, three powder compacts, a bedside light and two cigarette cases. A week earlier, my father had asked me what I would like and suggested a 'dressing case'. I said I would prefer a 'wireless', as we called them then, as there was none in the College, not even in the staff room. So he took me to an Oxford Street store where I chose one in black bakelite with a fretwork front. I remember that it cost £23, which was a lot of money. I have always been an avid listener (rather than a later viewer) and was eager to taste the delights of the new Third Programme, which had just started broadcasting. Besides classical music, it was the showcase for erudite drama and poetry, broadcasting writers such as T S Eliot and Dylan Thomas reading *Under Milk Wood*. The chief announcer was Alvar Lidell (such a sonorous name), chosen for his mellifluous Received Pronunciation tones. The lovely voice of Joy Worth added to our enjoyment. (Today's 'Radio 3' is a pale substitute.)

Next morning, I had a frantic call from Jinny. Both her own partner and that of her sister, Suzanne, had fallen through. Where, oh where were we to find two unattached men at such short notice? Our thoughts turned, inevitably, to Richard Vickers. He nobly suggested his twin brother Tom (whom we were all longing to meet) and one of his schoolmasters, Philip Mortimore-Bayley.

At last, the longed-for evening arrived and the classical beauty of Dial House was illuminated by a full moon. Inside sounds of music and merriment continued until the small hours. Most of my close Wren friends were there, Pam Wilson, Mary Bovill and her sister Julia. Audrey Wallin[8] brought a brilliant young naval officer, Peter White.[9] Jinny was delighted with her substitute partner and found Tom Vickers 'most attractive and much more flirtatious than Richard'. None of the other men stirred my heart. There were the local swains, Miche Balfour, Michael Goulder,[10] Dougal Kerr and Frank Tindall. The last-named, older than the others, had a crush on me (which was not reciprocated) and spent the evening telling me about 'reafforestation schemes in Windsor Park'. There was also 'Ping' (Ian Jamieson), minus the top of one finger which he had lost in a naval action that had earned him the DSC.[11] It was a wonderful, long-to-be-remembered evening. But one person was not there. Afterwards I wrote in my diary that 'I missed Peter like hell.'

I was just beginning to know my double cousin, Margaret, who was nineteen, the same age that my sister Peggy would have been. The following weekend we had been asked to a dance in Essex. Margaret had just learned to drive, and with great confidence we set out on a wild night with the rain and wind lashing the car. Suddenly, rounding a sharp bend in the darkness, we found ourselves in the ditch. There were no seatbelts in those days and I banged my head quite sharply on the windscreen. After a few minutes, a kindly lorry driver appeared and towed us out. The car stuttered on for a short distance and then gave up. Today, we would have whipped out our mobiles, but, hitching up our long skirts, we trudged on, eventually finding a red telephone box. We finally arrived at the dance at eleven o'clock. One of the first people we saw, on entering the house, was a neighbour of Margaret's, a languid Etonian called Julian Tennant who was draped over the piano. Exhausted with the trauma of the evening, Margaret exclaimed, 'Oh, Julian, how good to see you, I don't know anyone here.' He surveyed her from a great height. 'Oh,' he drawled, 'and who are YOU?' It was the ultimate put-down.

The weeks after my dance were an anti-climax. Jinny, Stella and I had returned to Holyport in low spirits and needed something to lift them. So we hatched a plot. Stella was avid to see Tom Vickers again, so she was deputed to write inviting him and Richard to join a party to see the ballet at Covent Garden. One morning, when I was having breakfast at the 'Staff' table, Stella waved a letter and winked at me from across the room. She gave me the 'thumbs up'. Amazingly, they would come. But we needed a third man – perhaps we could lure Peter Dallas Ross from his Burns Unit for the weekend. Again, it was Stella who wrote. It is difficult for younger readers to understand how limited were our means of communication: no mobiles, no texting and unreliable telephones. The only recourse was a letter or, if urgent, a telegram. Eventually we heard that Peter could come and I wondered what I would feel after an absence of two years.

When the longed-for day arrived, it was an anti-climax. Thick fog meant our swains could not drive us to London, so we had to go by train. After the ballet, in which Margot Fonteyn was dancing, we had planned to dine at Quaglinos and on to the Milroy, then the most fashionable nightclub. But the men had been unable to change (a dinner jacket was then obligatory for such places), so we had to make do with Boulestin's, a restaurant near Covent Garden. It was getting late, and the last Green Line bus had left, so we hired a car. The whole evening had been a disappointment. My emotions were not stirred by Peter, who seemed much more interested in Stella. She had fallen for Tom and reported later that he had been 'very hot stuff' in the car.

The year was at an end. I felt there was little to show for it and regretted my hasty decision to take the Holyport job. By the end of term, Jinny knew that she could stand the petty all-female world no longer. I, too, having started with high hopes, realised that the job was not for me. I was turning into a school-marm, invigilating exams and having to do every third weekend on duty. The atmosphere was frosty and formal, with staff addressing each other as Miss This and Miss That. Only with the cook, Mrs Arnott, a feisty war widow, did I feel at home. I wished that I had insisted on a term's trial.

* * *

Early in January 1947, I went up to Shropshire, where Mary Bovill, another Wren friend, had asked me to a hunt ball. Her family home, Mytton Hall, was a few miles north of Shrewsbury, and I loved the whole family. Her mother, widowed in such tragic circumstances,[12] was enormous fun, with a great sense of humour. On the Saturday before the dance, they gave a dinner party for twelve sprinkled with men from the Rifle Brigade and Hussars. Despite their light-heartedness, the Bovills were a deeply spiritual family and I learned much. Mary introduced me to T S Eliot, and in one of his verses from *Four Quartets* I found inspiration:

> I said to my soul, be still, and wait without hope
> For hope would be hope for the wrong thing; wait without love
> For love would be love of the wrong thing; there is yet faith,
> But the faith and the love and the hope are all in the waiting.
> Wait without thought, for you are not ready for thought:
> So the darkness shall be the light, and the stillness the dancing.

('East Coker')

There would be another eight years to wait.

* * *

Back in Holyport, life continued minus Jinny, whom I missed desperately. She had enrolled at a dancing school in London, with the idea of teaching. It was a spring of unparalleled savagery with deep snow and electricity shortages. On 7 February, Emmanuel Shinwell, the Minister for Fuel and Power, announced that the fuel situation was so grave that supplies to industry in the north-west and south-east would be cut altogether. On the 12th, things became even worse, as my diary records: 'The whole country is now cut off from 9-12 and from 2-4. Shops working by candlelight. Periodicals to be stopped – newspapers cutting down... factories stopping work all over the country.'

In February Jinny organised a party to the Chiddingfold Hunt Ball in Sussex. Unable to get a partner for me, we rang the inevitable Richard Vickers. I am amazed at how often we used him as a stopgap, and he was always pleased to come. He collected me from Orchard Cottage and we reached Wonersh in time for dinner. After the dance, we drove home, arriving at dawn. It was heaven to spend nine hours in his undivided company, and I longed to be gathered into his arms, but there was no spark. The devastating looks were skin-deep. Was he gay, or did he just not fancy me?[13]

In March, the headline news was of the floods that covered the country. Once more my diary reported: 'Bray is almost isolated with four feet of water and people are going about in boats. Some houses completely cut off. Dkws [Army transports known as Ducks] are being used in Maidenhead streets and swans swim in Oxford and Bedford.'

Living so close to Windsor, we were surrounded by Etonians. One of these was Duncan Balfour, whom some people found arrogant and overbearing, but who was always kind to me. A large man with a luxuriant ginger moustache, who always wore his OE tie, he had taken over from Charles Brooke as District Manager of Barclay's in Windsor. He and his French wife, Jeanne, had just moved into The Old House, a handsome eighteenth-century house next door to Clarence Lodge, where I had done my secretarial course. They had one son, Miche, who was my age and had recently come out of the RAF, where he had been an air gunner.

While The Old House was being refurbished, the Balfours had been living in the converted stables. This 'cottage' was now occupied by Sir George Bellew, Garter King of Arms, who was leaving to live in a Grace and Favour apartment at Windsor Castle. The Balfours offered it unfurnished to my mother, who was getting restless. Although Orchard Cottage had been our happy home for the past five years, we had missed our own furniture, stored for so long at Pettman's in Margate. Despite the heavy bombing of the Kent coast, it had survived undamaged. Now, at last, we could have our own things around us.

Old House Cottage had great charm. There was a small kitchen/dining-room downstairs, in the former stable; then up steep stairs to a handsome drawing-room and two bedrooms. We held our breath as the furniture arrived from Margate and the Sheraton bookcase just squeezed in by an inch. It made the room, which was also big enough to take the Queen Anne china cabinet, the mahogany tallboy and the oak chest.

We lived at fairly close quarters to the Balfours, for we were in their drive. I was rather in awe of Duncan, for he had a bullying manner and could be unkind about people. When we played tennis with them, I invariably served four double-faults. However, if one stood up to him, he mellowed. They were kind neighbours and we spent many happy evenings with them, playing bridge or listening to music. Miche, their son, was small, dark and very French.

Spring became summer, and I gave in my notice to Holyport. Three terms, I felt, were quite enough. The problem was, what was I going to do? I had always wanted to go to France and I decided to spend my £100 gratuity from the WRNS on a three-month course at a Paris finishing school. I went to see Gabbitas and Thring, the well-known educational consultants, who advised me to write to a Mademoiselle Vincent, who ran the sort of establishment I was seeking.

At the beginning of July, my father asked me to go up to London for something important. I couldn't imagine what it could be. When I arrived, he said he was taking me to meet his future wife!

I was amazed. I don't remember where we met Nancy Mason,

probably in her Highgate flat, but I liked her immediately: 'small-ish, plumpish and dark – about 38 – with a very jolly face'. My father was a different person – 'he actually did the washing up by himself!' Nancy was a feisty woman, a maths graduate from Birmingham University and an ex-rally driver. The family was in the leather business in that city and had clearly made money. She had a good sense of humour and obviously adored my father.[14] They had met while they were both working in the Ministry of Food. I was delighted that he was happy at last, after a dreary year living in digs.

* * *

It is 6.30 on Thursday 3 July. I am working late in the office at Holyport when the telephone rings. A male voice asks for 'Miss McNaughton'. 'Thinking it to be Miche, or possibly Ian Jamieson (for I could not mistake Richard's voice), I was not particularly excited. "This is Peter Dallas Ross speaking."' I was amazed, for I had not seen him since our ballet party before Christmas, when he had seemed to be much more enamoured of Stella than me. Quite why he transferred his allegiance to me, I never discovered.

He came to collect me within the hour, driving his father's big black Rover, and took me to Skindles, a famous riverside hotel in Maidenhead. After dinner we danced amorously and later went on the river in an electric canoe, which I found 'absolute heaven'. The next night, Friday, we drove up to London, to my cousin Beryl's twenty-first dance in Finchley. On Saturday evening we joined six of his friends at Oatlands Park Hotel, Weybridge: Winsome, his sister, whom I liked very much; her friends Rosemary Collings-Wells and Pat Reid, an old flame of Peter's; Pat's brother Donald; John Parbury, a neighbour, and David Chapman, an Oxford under-graduate, later an Eton beak (master). Afterwards, we went back to David's house at Wentworth, where we rolled back the carpet and danced. I was wearing quite a sexy black dress, which I had just bought at Harrods. David was 'very hot stuff' and said that 'I gave him ideas'. On Wednesday, which was Peter's last night at home (he was on leave from his post at the Birmingham Accident Hospital), we went back to Skindles. 'We touched on religion and I found that he inclines towards Buddhism, as I do.' Later, we took a boat on the river where he told me he loved me. Two years earlier, I had been praying for this to happen. Now that it had, I did not believe him, and told him so. I did not expect to hear from him again.

Two weeks later was the Holyport dance, the culmination of three terms' hard work. The big house was a perfect setting, with large gardens beyond. Stella and I had asked all the men we could think of, but neither Tom Vickers (for whom Stella had fallen in a big way) nor Ian Jamieson could come. Richard brought a fellow-schoolmaster, Philip Mortimore-Bayley, to augment the men. For once, my eyes and heart did not seek out the handsome aquiline features of Richard on the dance floor, for, to my great surprise, Peter turned up. He had written me one or two amorous letters and that evening told me many times that he loved me. I again told him he was talking nonsense.

It was the summer *Oklahoma!* was playing in London, and every dance band played 'People Will Say We're in Love'. I felt that it might be coming true.

In August, the country lurched into an economic crisis. Clement Attlee, the Prime Minister, broadcast to the nation, more food and petrol rationing was talked of, the tax on American films was increased (so no Hollywood films), and everyone aged between eighteen and forty had to register at the Employment Exchange in order to get a job. It was almost like wartime again. But, worst of all, the amount of sterling one could take out of the country was cut from £100 to £30. It looked as though my Paris adventure in September was off.

In the middle of August, my mother and I went to France. Apart from a day trip to Boulogne before the war, I had never crossed the Channel. It took us almost twenty-four hours to get to Brittany, where we were going to a hotel on the north coast. We travelled overnight on the ferry from Southampton to Saint-Malo, and, after a series of trains, changes, and local buses, arrived that evening in Perros-Guirec, a small fishing village. Friends had recommended us the Hôtel Les Feux des Iles. It was run by Monsieur Catieux, the chef/proprietor, who had cooked in all the best hotels – The Ritz, Claridges, and so on. After the exigencies of wartime, the food was delicious, and the meals, in typical French fashion, lasted for two or three hours. The only snag was that there were no baths or hot water – I don't recall why – and we felt very dirty. We were amazed how quickly France had recovered, only two years after the end of the war, and, despite their suffering, the gaiety and ebullience of the French people were an inspiration. Everywhere there was colour – brightly painted shops and cafés – the *pâtisseries* full of rich cream cakes – the people laughing and lighthearted. I fell in love with them at once: a love affair that would last all my life.

We returned to an England full of wartime austerity. The news was worse. As from 1 October, no money whatsoever would be allowed out of the country for pleasure travel abroad. I now wrote sadly to Mademoiselle Vincent, Madame La Directrice of the finishing school, to say that I would be unable to go. I was downcast, but had reckoned without French ingenuity. With typical French insouciance she replied, '*ça ira*'.[15] Exactly how, I would later discover.

Meanwhile, all the time I had been away, Peter had been writing to me constantly. While I had embarked on a lighthearted flirtation, he was becoming serious. He had had to cancel one weekend at home, as he had a seriously ill baby to look after. This was a big disappointment to us both, and I realised that my feelings were running away with me.

One Saturday in early September, I went down to Haslemere for the twenty-first dance of another Wren friend, Ingeborg Harmsworth, whose mother was Danish. Her father, Sir Alfred, was a rich newspaper magnate, and their house was opulent. Among the guests was an Anglo-French artist, John Edmunds, who was flirtatious and suggestive. He asked me out for an evening in London and I met him at the Hyde Park Hotel. He had shed his bohemian manner, appeared to be well-groomed and respectable, and confessed that his louche behaviour at the dance had only been a line for a party. We joined some friends and finished the evening drinking beer in a pub. I was a novice beer drinker and after a gin, followed by six half pints, felt the room spinning.

Peter's boss had ordered him to take the weekend off as he was exhausted, and on the Sunday after Inge's dance he arrived at Old House Cottage. We drove to Hurley, near Henley, and had lunch at The Olde Bell. There was an entirely different feeling in the air – no longer light flirtation but deep seriousness. We talked about children, and then he took me home to meet his parents. They lived at Dalkeith House, a handsome Regency house on the main Egham to Bagshot road, with a lovely garden. His father, a doctor, was a psychiatrist of about fifty-eight, and his mother, small and shy, was German. They received me with great warmth, and I felt that I was being welcomed into the family.

On 12 September, my father married Nancy at the Marylebone Register Office. The bride was nervous (it turned out that she was forty-two, not thirty-eight as I had thought), and when asked if her name was 'Nancibel Freda Mason'[16] collapsed into giggles which

My father and his new bride Nancy Mason, at their reception at Stanhope Place W1, 12 September 1947. Standing at the back are Kenneth Mason (brother) and John Serrell-Watts (brother in law). In the front row, from left to right are the bride's sisters Audrey Mason and Cynthia Watts; Stewart McNaughton (my father's brother); the bride and groom; Mrs Mason (the bride's mother); Jill McNaughton and Enid McNaughton (Stewart's wife).

Jack and Nancy, showing my father in unusually skittish mood – he has just stuck a sprig of heather down Nancy's cleavage.

lasted for the entire service. It was embarrassing, and I felt very sorry for her. The reception was at 6 Stanhope Gate, Park Lane, and my mother was furious to hear that Uncle Roland, now the 3rd Lord Airedale, had proposed the health of the happy couple. She thought that this was treachery, but Roland and Jack had always been good friends. Among the guests was my father's cousin Forbes, who ogled me roguishly.

Peter was hoping to come home for the week-end of the 20th, but at 8 o'clock on the Saturday evening, when I had changed into my pink silk evening dress, a telegram arrived. 'Dorothy [his House surgeon] ill. All hell reigns here. Cannot therefore come home. Furious and terribly disappointed. Love Peter.' It was miserable for us both. I rang him the following evening and was surprised to get hold of him. He was generally so elusive on the telephone. He had just finished giving a blood transfusion to a seriously ill baby. He said that Dorothy had suspected infantile paralysis – but, although she had all the right symptoms, he did not think this

The second marriage of my father's cousin Forbes to Violet Gamage c 1948. He, like my father, had the devilish McNaughton charm.

30

was correct. 'It is such hell – he had wangled a whole week off from yesterday! Probably fate is putting in a warning hand!'

The date of my departure for Paris drew near. In order to meet the 1 October deadline, after which no money could be taken out of the country, I was leaving on Monday 29 September. Dorothy had improved and Peter had managed to get the weekend off. On Saturday evening he took me up to London. We dined at a little French restaurant, Chez Fabri, on the Bayswater Road, and I realised that we had become very close. He told me that his engagement in 1945 would never have worked, as Betty Hume Wright was a Roman Catholic.[17] He also said that his parents' marriage had not been a great success. Later, we went on to the Milroy, his favourite nightclub. There, he asked me to marry him.

The two telegrams from Peter Dallas Ross announcing his arrival and then cancelling his visit. Telegrams were our usual means of communication for urgent messages – one paid by the word so messages were succinct.

Notes

[1] Nancy Knox and Sylvia Giddings, my mother's wartime paying guests. Nancy married Major John Holmes and Sylvia married Geoffrey Tennant. See volume 2 of my memoirs, *Not the Purser's Daughter?*, pages 103 and 110--11.

[2] *Not the Purser's Daughter?*, page 94.

[3] See the *Dictionary of National Biography* entry on the eighteenth-century novelist Susan Ferrier reproduced on pages 127–130 of *Call Back Yesterday*, the first volume of my memoirs.

[4] Later Lord Ballantrae.

[5] See *Not the Purser's Daughter?*, page 130.

[6] See *Not the Purser's Daughter?*, page 104.

[7] See *Not the Purser's Daughter?*, pages 83–5.

[8] See *Not the Purser's Daughter?*, pages 123–4.

[9] Later my husband's boss in the Admiralty (Naval Intelligence), he ended his career as an Admiral with a 'K'. See *Not the Purser's Daughter?*, page 137, note 21.

[10] An Etonian 'tug' (scholar) who became Professor of Biblical Studies at the University of Birmingham.

[11] See *Not the Purser's Daughter?*, pages 128, 130, 135, 138.

[12] See *Not the Purser's Daughter?*, page 131

[13] In 1960, aged forty-three and 'after what he called years of hesitant bachelordom' (*Daily Telegraph* obituary 21 January 2003), he married a glamorous Swiss girl, Verena Kung, who had joined the staff of the school and who bore him three children.

[14] She was to be a kind step-grandmother. With typical Jewish generosity, she left handsome gifts to Jack's grandchildren.

[15] 'We'll manage.'

[16] She hated the name Nancibel, and used to say that it reminded her of a cow.

[17] I had been devastated when I read it in *The Times* in October 1945 (see *Not the Purser's Daughter?*, page 130).

Chapter *2*

Paris

'And go well satisfied to France again.'

Love's Labour's Lost 2.1.152

At Victoria Station, underneath the sign saying 'To the Continent', lay the long, sleek, yellow train. Its name, the Golden Arrow, made the hairs prickle on the back of my neck. This was the biggest adventure of my life – to be travelling abroad, on my own, to France. It was Monday 29 September 1947, and there were only two more days before all foreign travel for tourists ceased. The economic situation in England had become so serious that travellers could not take more than £30 each out of the country. The Golden Arrow was packed. I sat opposite a fat man in thick pebble glasses, who said he was something hush-hush in the Ministry of Supply. He plied me with cigarettes, carried my coats through Customs at Dover, and stood me a drink on board the ferry, *Invicta*. I sat down to lunch next to a girl whose face was familiar, and found she was Jenny Mackintosh,[1] who had been at Benenden with my cousins.

At four o'clock we pulled into the Gare du Nord. She was waiting at the barrier as she said she would, a small, slight figure of about fifty, her faded blonde hair topped by a black pill-box hat, a white carnation, our agreed signal of recognition, in her buttonhole. This was Mademoiselle Vincent, *directrice* of the finishing school I was about to join

Briskly waving away a horse-drawn fiacre, saying it was much too expensive, she hailed a brawny porter in a pale blue blouson, who hoisted my heavy trunk on his shoulders. We followed him into the smoky, Gauloise-scented depths of the Metro, getting out at L'Europe, a short walk from Mamzelle's *appartement* at 40 Rue de Moscou. This was not the most chic part of Paris – that was the

33

The river Seine in Paris, taken by the author in 1953.

seizième, the 16th *arrondissement*.[2] We were in the 8th, which lies to the north of the Gare Saint-Lazare, and we could hear the engines shunting in the distance. The *quartier* was neither smart nor salubrious – it was rather like the area around Paddington. (Although the *huitième* also contained embassies and legations, the Rue de Moscou was on the northern edge of respectability.) The district had been developed after the Napoleonic Wars and the streets, which radiated from Place de l'Europe, bore names like Rome, Leningrad and Londres.[3] To the north lay Place Pigalle, the haunt of pimps and prostitutes, and shady nightspots like the Moulin Rouge.

Mamzelle's apartment was four floors up one of the tall houses which fronted the street, and the porter, by now puffing heavily, for there was no lift, dumped my trunk inside the front door. I paid him 250 francs (about ten shillings) gratefully. Mamzelle took only four students, and two of these had already arrived. They were all younger than me: Margaret Edwardes, eighteen, who lived in Nottingham, and Janet Saul, a raven-haired Jewish girl of seventeen.

The fourth, Rosemary Brown Douglas, who was twenty, appeared that evening. Others in the *appartement* were Eveline, who was French and who worked during the day, and Elizabeth Cecil, a sophisticated married friend of Mamzelle who had also come over on the Golden Arrow that day.

Years later, when reading Julian Critchley's irreverent memoir A Bag of Boiled Sweets,[4] I came across his account of his student days at the Sorbonne (admittedly after my time) and immediately recognised this establishment:

> We were convinced that there were many more English girls out there somewhere in Paris, living alone in dingy rooms or, if their parents were richer, lodging with several others in some smart house in the better suburbs under the strict supervision of an elderly Frenchwoman of irreproachable reputation. One such maison was believed to exist at 40 rue de Moscou in the 8th arrondissement. We nicknamed it 'the Kremlin' and set about the task of liberating its occupants.

Unfortunately, there were no such raiding parties in my day.

I was a little disappointed to be told that, as I was the oldest, I would not be living in the flat, but would have a room with a friend of hers, Madame Stern, on the floor below. However, I soon discovered the joy of privacy in which to read and work. I also had the use of a kettle with which to wash – the others had to manage with cold water. There was no shower so we 'strip-washed'. Once a week we went to the public baths nearby where we paid 20 francs (about one shilling). Although both Mamzelle and Madame Stern possessed baths, they kept them filled with cold water in case *les toilettes* refused to function due to the constant strikes – a horrifying thought.

Next morning, I awoke to the sound of street cries and looked out of my window. Below, cycling down the Rue de Moscou was a small man who shouted what seemed like '*eskimo*'. He was a knife-sharpener bearing his tools in a wooden box on wheels in front of him, rather like the Walls Ice Cream 'Stop Me and Buy One' before the war. I heard his voice at the same time each morning, and came to rely on him. There were other street vendors, musicians and organ-grinders, as well as 'rag and bone' men, whose cries I began to recognise.

The first day there were no lessons, and Elizabeth Cecil took me out to see the sights. I was in heaven, intoxicated with the sounds and smells and sheer *joie de vivre* of this marvellous city. We explored the main *boulevards*, some of the shops and the outside of the Madeleine church. Later, we met an Australian journalist friend of hers on the *Evening Standard*, who was writing a piece about 'The Last Tourist from England'. Elizabeth had her photograph taken, which appeared with the article the next day. (I did not then know that this was the legendary Sam White, the doyen of foreign correspondents for almost half a century, who held court in the bar of Le Crillon every day at noon.)

That evening, we started our preparation for the next day's lessons – a reading of Molière's *Le Bourgeois gentilhomme* – and I finished writing my diary at ten minutes to one.

Mamzelle's flat was not large. There was the *salon*, a dining-room and three or four bedrooms. Margaret and Janet shared a room, as did Rosemary and Eveline, so I soon realised my good fortune. The food was cooked by a large Polish woman called Denise who made wonderful apple fritters and spoiled us when Mamzelle was out.

Short, fair and voluble, Mamzelle was a small dynamo of energy. A gifted teacher, she worked us hard, determined that her charges should imbibe as much French civilisation as possible in three short months. Lessons were held every morning in the *salon*, where we huddled round the unpredictable stove; strikes were frequent and we would often be interrupted by Denise, yelling '*le gaz ne marche pas*' and bearing aloft a raw joint of beef which she placed optimistically on top of the stove. It was distracting to try to concentrate while our nostrils were filled with the delicious scent of sizzling beef.

Corneille's *Le Cid*, Racine's *Andromaque* and *Le Bourgeois gentilhomme* were our daily fare. Each evening we had to write an essay on the day's work and prepare for the morrow. We were left to work very much by ourselves, more like university, and here I found my small, quiet room a godsend. Mamzelle, a hard task-mistress, kept late hours, and it was often nearly one o'clock before I had finished. There was no time to be idle.

There was also Balzac to read for private study. I had been given *La Recherche de l'absolu*, a moralistic novel which, being pure philosophy, would have been difficult enough in English. However, with my burgeoning French, I was beginning to enjoy it. In addition, we had to absorb George Sand's *La Mare au diable* and Hilaire Belloc's *Marie Antoinette*. I also discovered French poetry. We read Lamartine, de Musset and Victor Hugo – his lament *A Villequier*, written after the death of his daughter, brought tears to my eyes, reminding me of Peggy. Reading in French was becoming easier now, helped by our frequent visits to the theatre, which at first I found very difficult to understand. My use of the language was still rudimentary, but having read and discussed each play aloud twice the previous day helped, though I still found the actors talked very fast. In the gilded splendour of the Comédie Française, a marvellous opulent extravaganza of the Second Empire with red plush seats and swags of swinging cherubs, we saw Racine's *Andromaque* and *Brittanicus*, Beaumarchais' *Le Barbier de Séville* and Balzac's *La Rabouilleuse*. This last was adapted from his novel and was a stirring drama of which I understood only the main points. We were, of course, not supposed to speak English, but sometimes, between ourselves, we slipped into our mother tongue. All French theatres ended very late, and we did not get to bed until after one o'clock.

A lesson we disliked was *le diction*, which was taken by Mlle Barrault, a retired actress from the Comédie Française.[5] She lived in a lovely eighteenth-century house known as *un hotel particulier* in the *quartier* of Paris called le Marais. Here, all the houses were venerable, as were most of their owners. Mlle Barrault was terrifying, a tall stately woman of great presence; each of us had to stand in her *salon* and declaim a piece we had learned by heart the previous week, while she tore our execrable accents to pieces. It was doubtless good for our souls and our command of the language but we were always delighted when *une grève* (a strike) of some sort prevented our lesson.

At an embassy drinks party, we had met Mme Ginette Spanier, *Madame la directrice de Pierre Balmain*, a recent arrival on the Parisian fashion scene. Entrée to the collections of the Top Ten designers

Christian Dior's 'New Look' which was sweeping Paris in the early 1950s.

was jealously guarded and tickets were scarce. We were therefore elated to receive an invitation from Madame Spanier a few days later. She greeted us at the top of the stairs of Balmain's eighteenth-century house near the Rond-Point on the Champs-Elysées, a tall and elegant figure in black. She was in charge of all the sales and attended personally to her clients' requirements. She told us, in excellent English, that some of the clothes being modelled would be sold for about £100 (a vast sum in those days), while others would cost a great deal more. (One of her most important clients was the Duchess of Windsor.) The air was heavy with Balmain's own *parfum.*⁶ and we sat on silver cane chairs surrounded by the most elegant women in Paris. Some had brought their poodles, and the wretched animals were stuffed under the chairs like tiny muffs. With typical *joie de vivre*, the French had apparently forgotten the four years of German occupation and were now in the mood for frivolity. Gone were the heavy, dull, serge clothes of wartime. No longer restricted by rationing, the couturiers let themselves go. Skirts were now full and flouncy, with hemlines only eight inches from the ground. The *mannequins*, their faces frozen with hauteur, strode down the narrow catwalk, a jacket or scarf flung casually over their shoulders.

Although the 'New Look', with its ankle-length hemlines, was sweeping Paris, many of Balmain's dresses reflected the lines of the pre-1914 and post-1918 periods. Most were so exaggerated that ordinary mortals like us would find few occasions to wear them. An exception was the evening dresses, the *robes du soir*, which were exquisite. Bouffant and feminine, they were made in the most delicate materials; yards of silk, chiffon, and all the flimsy, dreamy fabrics that had vanished for so long. I longed to own just one. On our return to the flat, the four of us immediately lengthened all our skirts – we were not going to be dowdy country cousins.

One of our lessons was *la couture* (dressmaking), for which we had to make our own patterns. Fired with enthusiasm by Balmain's lovely clothes, we decided to make ourselves cocktail dresses. At Galeries Lafayette I bought some yellow and cream material, decorated with grapes, apples and strawberries. The tutor, Madame Clocher, was appalled and said we were *idiots* to embark on something so complicated and that we should have begun on a simple item like *une blouse*. Rather shamefacedly we agreed.

Many friends had given me introductions, and one of these, Odette, took me round Paris. She showed me all the picture-postcard views, the Place de la Concorde, the Champs-Elysées, and the Eiffel Tower.

We often went to the theatre under Mamzelle's supervision, and were surprised to find how much we were beginning to understand. Corneille's *Le Cid* and Molière's *Le Misanthrope* were both enthralling. Once we attended a gala performance at the Opera, where the marble steps approaching the grand tier were lined with powdered flunkeys in a livery of scarlet and gold. Operas we saw included *Aida*, *Lohengrin*, *Romeo et Juliette* and *Tosca*.

One Sunday afternoon, a chap called Maurice arrived to take me out. I had been given his name by Margaret Silley, one of the staff at Holyport. He was not attractive, but kind and attentive. It was good for my French to practise speaking with all and sundry, and I found it was coming more easily now. He took me to Notre Dame, where a service was in progress. The combined effect of the organ and the incense was overpowering.

The following day Mamzelle took us to see the *Conciergerie*, the prison where Marie Antoinette was imprisoned during the Terror. We sat on the bench where she waited for the tumbril to take her off to execution and saw the actual steps and knife of the *guillotine*. Then we went to the Palais de Justice on the Ile de la Cité where the Revolutionary Council sat.

One Sunday morning we took the Metro to the Porte de Clignancourt to see the *marché aux puces*, the celebrated flea market founded in the Middle Ages by the rag and bone men of the city, who picked up anything they could find in the crowded streets. Here, among rows and rows of stalls, one could browse among everything from bric-a-brac, ribbons, zips, haberdashery and rubbish to the finest antiques. Anyone with a good eye could pick up a bargain. In such a raffish atmosphere, there were many thieves and pickpockets about, and we were told to wear our oldest clothes and look as poor as possible.

One of Mamzelle's ploys to help our French was to ask her young friends to come and talk to us in the evening. There was a *quid pro quo* – we would teach them English. The first arrival was a young doctor, Pierre Bour, who was about thirty. He was short and dark, with a look of Cary Grant, and I found him quite attractive. The plan was that he would come twice a week, alternating the languages. The other three students had all been allocated girls — the cachet of having a man had been given to me as I was the oldest. He was an intern in a hospital some way out of Paris and sometimes took me out there on the back of his motorbike – an exhilarating experience.

Paris was in political turmoil and strikes were frequent. Both the Metro and the buses were often out of action, and electricity was sometimes cut from seven in the evening until six the next morning. The most unpleasant strike was by the dustmen. The *pubelles*, with their stinking contents, remained in the streets for days. Municipal elections were imminent, and there was fear of a general strike if the communists won. There was much street fighting, with the *communistes* bursting the tyres of buses. Mamzelle was reluctant to let us go out at night. In the event, General de Gaulle's new party, *Le Rassemblement du Peuple Français*, was elected, not the communists.

As part of our education, various tutors took us to see the sights: the Eiffel Tower, Montmartre, the Sacré Coeur – all were included. Another day, we walked round Le Marais, one of the oldest *quartiers* in the 4th *arrondissement*, containing sixteenth- and seventeenth-century houses, one of which had belonged to Madame de Sévigné, author of the famous seventeenth-century letters, which was now a museum. One of the most magical places was the Sainte-Chapelle, on the Ile de la Cité. Built by Louis IX in 1248 to house the relics of the Passion, it is one of the architectural glories of the western world. Many of the priceless stained-glass windows had been removed for safe-keeping during the war and had not yet returned. Even so, its ethereal beauty and blue star-spangled ceiling were unforgettable.[7] Another time, we visited the Archives, housed in the beautiful eighteenth-century Hôtel de Rohan. We saw the verbatim account of the trial of Jeanne d'Arc, letters of Louis XIV, the last letter of Marie Antoinette, and the death warrant of Louis XVI.

At weekends, longer excursions were made by train. We saw the lovely little Château de Chantilly, home of Prince Louis II de Bourbon, known as le Grand Condé, a famous military commander in the reign of Louis XIV. Another time we went to Chartres. The great cathedral stands on a hill above the town, its outline a landmark for many miles. We were lucky enough to be shown round during High Mass, the rose windows lit by the setting sun, while the great organ played a Bach fugue in the background.

The massive grandeur of Versailles enthralled us with its classical statues and fountains decorating the formal park. Here we saw the Petit Trianon, a charming little house where Marie Antoinette entertained her close friends. We were shown the dining-room with its table which rose or fell at the touch of a hidden spring so that Her Majesty's secret assignations were undisturbed by the entry of servants. Some distance away in the park was the rustic farmhouse where the Queen played at being a shepherdess in a vain attempt to forget the rising clamour of the Revolution.

One of the most memorable parts of our visit to Versailles was *Le Spectacle de son et de lumière* that brought its history to life. As soon as the pale sun had faded from the evening sky, the great rose-bricked palace was illuminated by a thousand floodlights, some pink, some white, some yellow. Majestic music thundered from hidden microphones, and the voice of Jean Cocteau began to tell the timeless story. The footsteps of Louis XIV, the glorious Sun King, were heard stumping along the corridors. At the same time, the flickering lights picked out his progress from the far side of the

Palace until they reached the central chamber. '*Messieurs, Le Roi*': a fanfare of trumpets announced his presence. The most exciting sequence was the arrival of the revolutionaries from Paris in 1789, intent on seizing the royal family. The animal roars of the mob were heard in the distance, growing louder and more ferocious as they approached the Palace gates: '*La Reine, La Reine, à bas La Reine*'. Panic-stricken feet raced along the corridors to flee the furious vengeance of the people. One by one, the lights went out. But there was no escape. At last, only a single room remained illuminated. A woman's voice was heard to plead, '*mes enfants, sauvez mes enfants*'. Then that light, too, went out. The palace was plunged in darkness and all was still.

* * *

I had now been in Paris for five weeks and had had one short letter from Peter. My mother wrote constantly, and letters seemed to be getting through despite the strikes. (Letters were censored in England because of the currency restrictions, and many were opened to search for hidden pound notes.) The silence from Peter I found hard to bear, and I wondered whether I was falling in love with him. I knew I was not, but yearned to hear from him. At last, on 4 November, I had a proper letter. His boss and his house surgeon had both been ill and he had been running the unit, looking after thirty badly burned children, single-handed.

On 18 November, I celebrated my twenty-second birthday. Peter sent me a bunch of red carnations,[8] and Mademoiselle gave me a handkerchief with a card which said '*Pour que vous trouviez bientôt l'élu de votre coeur*'.[9] Not soon, but seven years to wait.

Tiny though she was, Mademoiselle possessed a colourful vocabulary and extremes of temperament. She could be *formidable* when roused. One evening, when I was fiddling with her elderly wireless, trying to change channels, all the lights went out. I had created *une panne*. '*Misérable créature*', she shrieked, rolling every one of her rrrs. As we were often in darkness, owing to the power cuts, this was not a popular move. Candles were produced, and I felt chastened. It took some time for the antiquated wiring in the apartment to be repaired, Later, she relented and I again became *'un chat noir'*, a term of great endearment.

One evening we told Mamzelle that we had tickets for the Folies Bergères. She threw up her hands in horror and said that we could not possibly visit such a place unchaperoned. We pleaded, and, as four of us were going together, she relented. Strict instructions were given. We were to remain in our seats throughout the performance. On no account were we to wander in the foyer during the intervals. This was somewhere no *jeune fille bien élevée*[10] was ever seen. The evening was uneventful – no old men in seedy raincoats tried to pick us up, or young ones, for that matter – and we felt somewhat let down.

Our visits to the Musée du Louvre remain in my mind as one of the glories of those months, and the appetite, once whetted, compelled one to return again and again. Leonardo's Mona Lisa, and the works of Raphael, Rembrandt and El Greco were a revelation. I also discovered modern art and the Impressionists, Renoir, Monet, Manet and Degas. There were artists I did not know, like Vlaminck, de Segonzac and Utrillo. But the greatest revelation was sculpture. I had never heard of Rodin and was overwhelmed with the lyrical beauty of his figures locked in pre-coital ecstasy. I gave an illustrated catalogue to my father for Christmas, and he was shocked to the core of his Calvinistic soul. He snapped it shut, saying that it was 'disgusting'.[11]

Money was a constant worry. I foolishly bought some silver *lamé* material to make an evening dress, and although it was much cheaper (and very much more glamorous) than anything I could have bought in England, it was still an extravagance I could ill afford. The five metres cost me 3,605 francs – about £7 or two weeks' salary of a secretary. Two weeks later, doing my accounts, I realised my folly. I had only £8 left to last till the end of term, and out of that had to pay the art teacher and the *couture* woman, as well as tips and things. There was only one answer. Go to the spivs. We were all smokers, and had each brought a supply of cigarettes to last out the term. Although they were intended for smoking, they were also hard currency on the *marché noir*. One only had to go to the

Place Madeleine, which was the haunt of the black marketeers. Here all the spivs congregated, ready to pounce upon English girls who had cigarettes to sell. One of them said that his mother worked in the nearby ladies' lavatory – *la toilette* – and would be happy to do business. Down I descended and found the old woman who was the attendant. After a bit of bartering, she agreed to buy two packets of twenty for 260 francs, about ten shillings, which was a help.

In early December, our families at home were reading alarming reports of the crisis in France. Everyone seemed to be on strike – trains, buses, post, water. The electricity was cut several times a day. Denise, the cook, announced that *les communistes* had sabotaged one of the main electricity stations and that only two remained to service the whole of Paris. Theatres closed. There were frightening photographs of rifles stacked in barricades in the Parisian streets, reports of troops standing by at Versailles and headlines in the English papers: 'Another French Revolution?', 'Civil War in France'. The new Prime Minister, Monsieur Schuman, ordered drastic action and was about to declare a state of emergency. Our mothers, alarmed, were on the point of ordering us home. As quickly as it began, everything cooled down. The strikers agreed to go back to work, leaving the overflowing dustbins stinking on the streets.

At last, on 18 December, this great adventure came to an end. I returned to England, a different person, honed and polished by French civilisation, having discovered the joy of learning for its own sake .

My Parisian diary ends with the words '*Tu ne me chercherais pas, si tu ne m'avais pas trouvé.*'[12]

My quest for truth had just begun.

Notes

1 She subsequently married Simon Fraser, one of the Lovats of Beaulieu clan.
2 The equivalent of SW3 or SW7, where I later lived.
3 I have my street map and Plan de Paris, purchased in 1947, in front of me.
4 London, Faber, 1994. Julian Critchley was a backbench Tory MP (1959–64 and 1970–97) who could not stand Mrs Thatcher (he once described her as 'the label on a can of worms').
5 Probably a relation of the celebrated actor Jean-Louis Barrault, who had just had a great success with the film *Les Enfants du Paradis*.
6 I still use one – *Ivoire*.
7 On their return to Paris, in 1953, these windows, *les vitrines*, were displayed in the Louvre, before being put back in their rightful place, an exhibition I was lucky enough to see.
8 I still possess one. When I returned home, he gave me a silver powder compact, which I still have.
9 'Hoping that you will soon find the prince of your heart'.
10 Well-brought-up girl.
11 No wonder my poor mother suffered from his indifference in bed.
12 'You would not be seeking Me if you had not already found Me.' Blaise Pascal, *Mystère de Jésus*, quoted by Paul Bourget in his novel *Le Disciple*.

The marriage of my cousin Cynthia Sheill (twenty-one) to Lieutenant Aubone St Vincent Hammick ('Spike') Royal Navy (twenty-two), 19 August 1948 at Hampstead parish church.

Chapter 3

Rootless

'Extremely stretch'd and conn'd with cruel pain'

A Midsummer Night's Dream 5.1.80

After three months in Paris, where I learned to speak, write and read French with a fair degree of fluency, it was now time to face two hard decisions.

The most pressing need was to find a job. My mother made no secret of her loneliness and I decided that I must live at home rather than in London. Although I would have been much better paid had I chosen to work in the commercial field, I veered towards a literary future. Books, after all, were in my blood although I was unconscious of the fact. After a number of flirtations with publishing, all of which proved abortive, I was accepted by the British Council. Its London headquarters were in a handsome house in Grosvenor Square. This was a semi-government outfit that ran many projects worldwide supporting education, the arts, science and sport, including English libraries in most major cities abroad. I felt I had found my feet. I was put into the 'Periodicals Department', which sent a wide variety of trade journals all over the world. My boss, Miss Farrand, was a plain, humourless spinster in her forties who told me that 'a good secretary never makes mistakes.' Very soon, I got itchy feet and applied for a transfer to the Fine Arts Department, but was told I would have to wait.

Early in March, I answered an emergency call from my father. Nancy's mother was having a serious operation in Birmingham: would I go and look after him while she was away? I quite enjoyed the experience of cooking and keeping house, but, although he did his best to be charming, I felt we had little in common.

My second decision, of course, concerned Peter. We had had a wild and wonderful evening at the Chelsea Arts Ball at the Albert Hall on New Year's Eve, when I went as a Spanish dancer and he as a surgeon in operating kit. When he had asked me to marry him in September, I told him that our three months' courtship was far too short and that we did not really know each other. Recalling a fractured childhood in which raised voices and harsh words were the norm, I was determined that my marriage should last. It was with these doubts in mind that I had received my first proposal.

It was clear that a crisis was approaching. Not wishing to string him along and get all I could out of him, I felt that I had to be honest and told him that I had no intention of marrying him. 'Never?' 'No, never.' He did not seem to be unduly concerned and we continued to go out together. He returned to Birmingham where he was working desperately hard as a surgeon in the understaffed Burns Unit. In those days, junior doctors could be on call for forty-eight hours without a break, and Peter was often in sole charge of thirty badly burned people. The previous November, after Guy Fawkes' Night, he had spent twenty-four hours without leaving the theatre (something I did not discover until well over sixty years later, as I was drafting this chapter). Having had no letter for what seemed a long time (it was in fact ten days) and egged on by my mother, I wrote what I describe as a 'snorting' letter, expressing my disappointment. Silly little fool, wanting to have her cake and eat it. In my youth and naivety I failed to understand the stress under which he worked. (It is difficult, in the twenty-first century, to understand how marooned we were. There were no mobiles, text messages or email, and Peter was not allowed to use the hospital telephone for personal calls.) Months passed. In July I met his father in the village: 'Who do you think blew in last night?' I stayed in all that weekend, hoping he would call, but there was silence. I wrote in my diary that only French allowed me to express the depths of my despair: '*j'étais complètement écrasée*' (I was completely crushed).

On 6 August, I caught the bus to Egham station. At Royal Holloway College, a tall, familiar figure got in and sat down beside me. Peter!! I had waited for this moment for six long months, and

48

now that he was really here I could hardly believe it. We travelled up to London together. He kissed me goodbye, and said that he would definitely be coming to Stella Brooke's twenty-first dance in September.

Meanwhile, I had been getting steadily more bored at the British Council. Jinny Wyllie and her sister Suzanne had been sharing a flat in Cambridge, and when they said they were giving it up at the end of August I felt that I must make a move. (Suzanne was marrying Stephen Casey, her doctor fiancé, in September.)[1] My cousin Margaret also had itchy feet, and we decided to try our luck in Cambridge. I wrote to various bookshops and publishers, including Heffer's in Petty Cury. The head of this family firm was the seventy-year old William Heffer, large, and avuncular. He greeted me warmly and said that, as my letter had come 'as a bolt from the blue' (which intrigued him), he would offer me a job. At the same time there was a vacancy in the Cambridge office of the British Council, which was offered to Margaret. All was set for our latest adventure.

Rereading my diaries, I am appalled at how rootless I was, never settling in a job for more than six months, and falling in and out of puppy love with reckless ease. Perhaps it was the fragility of my home life. The burden of being an only child ('you're all I've got') and of being batted to and fro between my indigent parents, who seemed unable to manage their lives without me, was depressing. At the time, I never questioned my solitary role, but looking back from a distance of half a century I realise how exploited I was. Margaret's parents had had a long and fruitful marriage, and I envied her the stability of her home and family.

* * *

The lure of Cambridge was not academia, it was men. Like most of my friends educated in single-sex schools, we were man-mad. Ahead lay a magical year, in which four of us would find love. While I had much longer to wait, there were other gems: biking to work on a dappled autumn morning, the air full of bells; misty evenings punting on the Cam; serious talk in cloistered courts examining,

Pages from my diary, 25 March 1946. (The extract is reproduced on page 70.[2])

with gifted minds, the problems of the world; May Week madness, madrigals on the Backs, a job among books which I loved. But beyond it all, I matured, finding in music an undiscovered country – the brilliance of Mozart, the song of flute and 'cello, the majesty of Bach. Ten months later, the dream ended when the hounds of conscience dragged me home.

All this lay ahead as Margaret and I began our life together that August day. Number 53 Chesterton Road (now part of the Arundel House Hotel) overlooked the placid Cam and Jesus Green. Our first-floor flat contained a sitting-room and a double bedroom. Here we entertained in a rudimentary fashion. We had the use of a kitchen halfway down the stairs, and one evening, wishing to boil both potatoes and gooseberries, I thought I would save gas by cooking them together. The two young men who were our guests wrinkled their noses, but made no comment.[3]

Nine days after I started my new job, a telegram arrived from my mother: 'Feel ill. Fear operation. Please come.' Although I had been there for such a short time, Mr Heffer generously told me to catch the next train home. I found her in bed, in pain, being looked after by her 'daily'. Her doctor thought it was gall bladder and said he would get her into the cottage hospital. Two days later she was pronounced fit, and I hoped to return to my job in Cambridge.

For many months, my mother had been continuing her amorous correspondence with 'K', her Canadian lover, and he was shortly coming over to see her. She was working herself into a nervous frazzle, not having seen him for twenty years, and this probably accounted for her psychosomatic state. Added to which, she was letting our flat to friends for three months. She did not feel up to clearing it up for their arrival, and said she needed me for another week.

Meanwhile, the date of Stella's dance drew near, and I had had no word from Peter Dallas Ross. In June, I had spent a week in Perthshire with Elizabeth Irwin while Angus was away on a course. She was expecting a baby in August. I had poured out to her the story of my non-love-life with Peter, and she decided to do something about it. She knew of a young man in the Scots Greys, stationed at Aldershot, whom she thought I would like. One evening, when I was working late at the British Council, Peter Wagstaff rang and asked me to dinner. Three days later, we met at a little restaurant, Trio's, in Curzon Street. He was standing outside, a tall attractive figure in his late twenties, resplendent in tartan trews. We found that we had much in common and spent the evening talking about music, art, Rodin and Peter Abelard. I had recently been reading Charles Morgan's *The Fountain*, in which the hero, Lewis, had all the traits I most admired. Peter was an artist and had been a prisoner in Germany for five years with Angus. Here was someone with whom I was mentally attuned.[4]

What happened next fills me with shame, and I am appalled that

51

I could have behaved so callously. Stella's dance (for which Frank Saunders once more generously lent Dial House in Englefield Green) was on 18 September and neither she, nor I, had had any word from Peter. I decided that I could not be left without a partner, and asked Peter Wagstaff, who accepted, rather to my surprise. I had become close friends with Winsome, Peter Dallas Ross's sister, who asked me to stay at their home, Dalkeith House, as my mother had let our flat. On the evening of the 18th, while I was a guest in his house, Peter Ross 'blew in' unannounced. I realised that there were shoals ahead. Peter Wagstaff had been put up by friends, and the six of us met for dinner at the Ross's. I had explained the situation to Winsome and she had asked a friend of hers, Jessica Horniman, as Peter's partner. Jessica's brother, Michael, was Winsome's partner. The evening was complicated. I realised how shallow my feelings were for Peter D R, to whom I was very cool, and thought that I had found my ideal in Peter W. After the dance at Dial House, the six of us went on to the Milroy, where Peter D R told me that he had had a 'bloody' letter from me in February, when he had been without sleep for three days.[5] On receiving it, he promptly tore it up. I felt ashamed. It was, of course, the end. My only plea in mitigation was that I had at least been honest with him and told him that I had had no intention of marrying him.

Looking back, it was a close-run thing. Had Peter W not appeared on the scene, I would have fallen into Peter D R's arms, and would probably have married him. If he had come to see me when he was home in July or got in touch after we met in August, I would never have asked Peter W. Three days after Stella's dance, I had a charming letter from Peter W, who wrote that 'if he said he had enjoyed himself on Saturday, it would be an understatement'. I mistakenly took this as a personal compliment, for we had lunched together on the Sunday, and I had found him even more attractive and *sympathique*. He asked me to stay at his home one weekend, so I was glad that I had not jeopardised my chances with him by flirting with Peter D R. Much later, I discovered how devious had been the ramifications of that evening. While Peter D R was pining for me, I was longing for Peter W, who had fallen heavily for Jessica. He pursued her for many months afterwards but she, apparently, found him very *pi*.[6] *La Ronde* indeed.

I was convinced that at last I had found '*l'élu de mon coeur*',[7] and began a poem to him, in the style, so I imagined, of T S Eliot:

> *Somehow one knows when one reaches the end of the journey,*
> *The questing is done, the immeasurable distance is spanned.*
> *Here, all is peace and the waiting is sure.*

At last, having settled my mother and sorted out the flat, I could return to Cambridge and my job. Heffers generously paid me for my fortnight's absence. Although Margaret and I had long been friends (she was the only one of my twenty-four cousins to whom I felt close – at that stage, her sister Alison was too young), I had always thought of her as unsophisticated and not particularly pretty. In my patronising way, I looked on her as a younger sister, the same age as Peggy. It was therefore with some surprise that I found that this blonde and willowy girl had become a beauty whom most men found irresistible. (Looking at the photograph of our mutual McNaughton grandmother, it is clear from whom she inherited her looks.)[8] Among the young bloods who paid her court were Ian Lloyd, a twenty-seven-year-old South African who had been President of the Union the previous year;[9] and the smooth, handsome Tony Bullock, Trinity and the Life Guards, who became a diplomat. Another who was very taken with her was George Porter,[10] a postgraduate scientist at Emmanuel who soon afterwards became engaged to Stella. (Although some ex-servicemen were still doing their degrees, the majority of students were in their early twenties, and, at the vast age of twenty-three myself, I found most of them pretty young.)

One evening, about a month after our arrival, Margaret came home with shining eyes. 'I've met the most wonderful man.' 'What's his name?' 'Hugh Browne.' Very soon they became inseparable and it was clear that this was serious. Hugh, a Sapper, who had been ADC to General Brian Robertson in Germany, was twenty-five and reading engineering at Trinity Hall.

Among my admirers was a young man called John Gayer Anderson whose father was a renowned Egyptologist. (He left the contents of his Cairo house, Beit al-Kritliyya, to King Farouk who, in return, made him a Pasha. It is now the Gayer-Anderson Museum – much of his collection is in the Fitzwilliam Museum, Cambridge.) John practised sophisticated seduction of a kind I had not met before. He asked me to tea in his rooms and, to a background of Brahms' Fourth, read some of John Donne's most erotic poetry. It was heady stuff, but I did not succumb.

Another older ex-service undergraduate was John Turbott, who was reading Russian at Trinity. An RAF pilot, he had been shot down in the German-occupied Soviet Union, where he had been imprisoned. His tutor was the White Russian émigré Prince Obolonsky. John lived next door and was very musical. We would go and listen to him playing Beethoven's Appassionata Sonata and singing ribald Russian songs. He had a recording of Chaliapin singing 'Blaga' or 'the Song of the Flea'. I can still hear John's melodious bass voice accompanying him. He took me to many concerts, and we heard Solomon, a virtuoso pianist who had been a protégé of Grandfather Airedale,[11] and also Benno Moiseiwitsch. I also discovered the violin, an instrument that moved me with delight. I heard unforgettable performances of the Tchaikovsky, Mendelssohn and Brahms concertos, played by Ginette Neveu[12] and Gioconda de Vita.

My mind, atrophied at school, began to flower. Music was a dimension of the spirit that I had never imagined existed. Neither of my parents was musical – their tastes ranged from Ivor Novello to Gilbert and Sullivan – so I had never heard good music before. Margaret and I joined CUMS (Cambridge University Musical Society), which was conducted by Boris Ord, the fiery and idiosyncratic organist of King's College, legendary among his peers. We were rehearsing Bach's *St Matthew Passion*, which we would perform in King's chapel in March.

I was in heaven. Never before had I had such a wonderful time. Margaret was as sweet-natured as she was beautiful and we were very happy together. We hardly ever had an evening in, or if we did,

Jill and Ian Crichton (left – a short-lived boy friend) enjoying a joke at the Medical Society Ball, Cambridge, December 1948. She is wearing the silver lamé strapless evening dress that she made in Paris.

scarcely got to bed before midnight. On the rare occasions we had managed to turn in by eleven, someone would call, find us in curlers, and whisk us off to a dance.

My mother, having let the flat, was at a loose end. On 19 October, she arrived to stay for three weeks. She had had her fling with 'K', which was, unsurprisingly, not a success.[13] Two people living on twenty-five-year-old memories and sustained only by passionate, erotically charged letters felt anti-climax when the actual moment arrived. He had booked a service suite in King Charles II Street, St James, where they were to stay for several nights. Although he ordered oysters and champagne, the aphrodisiac did not work. He departed for Canada, and they never saw each other again.

Elizabeth Irwin had given birth to a son at the end of August, and asked me to be a godmother. Alistair Stuart Hastings Irwin was christened at St Stephen's, Rochester Row on 5 November. The vicar, the Reverend George Reindorp, was a tall, charismatic man of thirty-seven with great charm and sex appeal. He enjoyed, and encouraged, his society connections. I little knew that he would marry me in that church seven years later.[14]

The chief godmother, who held the baby, was Ros Pilcher, whom I had met when I stayed with Liz in June. She and her husband, Graham, shared the house with the Irwins. She told me that she had written several short stories for racy women's magazines and got her ideas while doing the washing up. A Wren, she had had lots of boyfriends and used her experiences as fodder for the magazines. Half a century later, as Rosamunde Pilcher, the world-famous novelist, she is a multi-millionaire.

I was still carrying a torch for Peter Wagstaff who was there as proxy godfather. I knew nothing of his passion for Jessica, and, while he was perfectly friendly, I realised that I had no place in his future.

It was five years since my confirmation preparations had been so suddenly aborted due to the molestations of an over-sexed naval padre,[15] and I decided to try again. On 9 December I was confirmed in Cambridge. I was filled with religious zeal, and the weight of my mother's loneliness began to burn into my conscience. I knew that, if she needed me, I should have to go.

Despite the ups and downs of my love life, I was enjoying my job. My main task was to write the 'blurbs' of new books for the forthcoming catalogue, and my horizons broadened. I discovered writers such as Kafka and Joyce, and others of whom I had never heard. From time to time, when they were short-handed, I was asked to serve in the shop. This was enormous fun. Undergraduates poured in from all sides, most of them to chat or flirt rather than buy books. I was also called on to work in the music department upstairs, which sold scores. Well-known musicologists such as Thurston Dart and Boris Ord were frequent visitors.

On Christmas Eve I was given a ticket for the King's Carol Service by John Guy, one of the choral scholars. This was a joyous uplifting of the spirit which I shall long remember. My mother and I spent Christmas at Roycot. Once again, Stewart and Enid, my uncle and aunt, had gathered in the lost sheep.

* * *

At the beginning of January 1949, Jinny decided to return to

Cambridge and took the single room next to our flat. My fears that three would be a bad number were groundless – nothing could have been more delightful. She and Margaret became close (and lifelong) friends. Jinny, who had been teaching dancing in London, now decided to open a school of her own in Cambridge. Many of the undergraduates had no idea how to dance, an essential if one wanted to attract girls. One of her first pupils was Anthony Lowe, a wartime Naval Officer of twenty-seven reading agriculture at Queens'. Jinny had been briefly engaged to Bob Fraser-Mackenzie, of Trinity, an amusing Highland Scot, but that quickly came to an end once she had met Anthony.

In March came our performance of *St Matthew Passion* in King's chapel. The ethereal beauty of the music as our voices soared into the fan vaulting will stay with me for ever.

Although I went home every third weekend, my mother was lonely. She had neither the gift nor the mental resources to live alone. Now in her mid-fifties, she yearned for a man. I was deliriously happy in Cambridge, but my conscience, softened by confirmation and a new religious zeal, goaded my guilt. In the middle of March, on one of my visits home, she confessed that she longed to have me back. I felt that my duty was clear and gave three months' notice to Heffer's. Years later, when my perspicacious husband enlightened me, I recognised the emotional blackmail for what it was.

In April, I lost my diary in the street. On going to the police station two weeks later, where it had been handed in, I was greeted with suppressed giggles from the policemen in charge. On the back page I had made a list: 'Eligible Bachelors, 1949 –NB The Cream only! (A pretty creamy lot!)'.

Cambridge was full of repartee and wit, much of it ribald. A ditty of the time, composed by a jilted lover, ran thus:

> There was a young woman called 'Sheena',
> Whose morals had never been cleaner,
> But the fact of the matter,
> Since Hayward got at her,
> That 'Sheena is now a 'Has Beener'.[16]

Early in May, my father went into Westminster Hospital for an operation. Like King George VI, he was suffering from hardening of the arteries, atherosclerosis, the result of heavy smoking and of gas in World War I. He made a good recovery and went off to a convalescent home.

Later that month, Winsome Dallas Ross rang me at home to tell me that Peter was engaged to be married. His fiancée was a nurse of about twenty-five in the same hospital. At last, I could begin to put him out of my mind.

The friendship between my cousin Margaret and Hugh Browne ripened, and on 10 June they announced their engagement. I felt that our Cambridge life was drawing to a close. Winsome Dallas Ross, too, was soon to be married to Jimmy Wilcox, a young man who was a clerk in the House of Commons. In August, Stella would marry George Porter. One by one, my friends were disappearing.

I had been to many dances, but with no one special. Term was drawing to an end, and people would be 'going down'. (One of my swains was John Thomson whose father, Sir George Thomson FRS, would become Master of Corpus Christi in 1952; John became a distinguished diplomat and High Commissioner to India in 1977. But there was no spark on my side.) But first came the 'May Balls', riotous formal occasions when girls wore their prettiest dresses and went with the man of their dreams. I had no such man in tow. Most of my friends had had invitations. I had not. It was therefore with some excitement that I received a letter from Miche Balfour, asking

me to the 'Commem' Ball at 'The House' (Christ Church), Oxford's most prestigious college. At last I had something to crow about.

The previous summer, Miche and I had had a brief flirtation when he had taken

Miche Balfour, with whom I was intermittently in love, aged twenty-one, at Versailles in 1946.

me to the summer dance at The Lodge, Holyport. He was small, dark and Gallic-looking, with all the finesse of his countrymen in the art of *l'amour*. I travelled to Oxford by train, and he put me up in digs near Merton. There were eight in the party, including Rachel Buxton, a friend of Alison's from Benenden, and Anthony Sampson, later to be a distinguished writer.[17] We danced in Christ Church's splendid Hall and wandered dreamily in Tom Quad. Later we took a punt on the river. I found him attractive but knew that I meant nothing to him. The fact that my mother was his parents' tenant and that we lived side by side made things more difficult.

In July, I left Cambridge for good. In the ten months of my stay I had learned much about life and art. As yet, I had not discovered the tender lyricism of Schubert nor scaled the cerebral heights of Bach. It was a young man's town, and already I felt old.

Rootless, feckless, jobless and manless, I felt as though I were cast adrift upon the world. My yearning for a husband and children was almost overwhelming. My son would be called Toby and my daughter, Catriona.

* * *

But first there were three weddings. On 23 July, Peggy Johnson became the wife of Peter Dallas Ross at Christ Church, Virginia Water. Her parents had died, so the wedding was given by the groom's family. My mother told me afterwards that Dr Ross had said to her, 'although we love Jill, a medical wife would be more helpful to his career, as he is so brilliant.'

Stella's wedding to George Porter at Holy Trinity, Brompton on 12 August was moving and beautiful. They used John Donne's lovely prayer, which I later included in my husband's funeral service and would like for my own:

> The God of Heaven so join you now, that you may be glad of one another all your lives. And when He which hath joined you, shall separate you, may he again stablish with you an assurance that He hath but borrowed one of you for a time to make both more perfect in the Resurrection.[18]

The marriage of Dr Peter Dallas Ross to Margaret Johnson, 23 July 1949. From left to right: the bride's aunt and uncle; Winsome Dallas Ross (sister); the groom and bride; best man and bridesmaid; Dr and Mrs Dallas Ross.

Invitation to the wedding of Peter Dallas Ross.

Jilly, a guest at Peter Dallas Ross' wedding.

Dr. and Mrs W. Dallas Ross
request the pleasure of

The Hon. Mrs. D. McNaughton & Miss Jill McNaughton

company at the marriage of

Margaret Jean,

daughter of the late Mr and Mrs E. W. Johnson,

to their son

Dr. Peter Dallas Ross,

at Christ Church, Virginia Water,

on Saturday, 23rd July, 1949,

at 3 o'clock,

and afterwards at Dalkeith House.

Dalkeith House,
Englefield Green,
Egham, Surrey.   R.S.V.P.

60

George was undoubtedly brilliant, and adored Stella. She looked lovely. They had a very happy marriage.

And then, on 3 September, Margaret married Hugh at Stansted Parish Church. A large dinner-party the night before consisted mainly of all the aunts and their spouses. Margaret looked ethereal, in a cream brocade wedding-dress made at Hartnell's by cousin Joyce, who was working there. I was one of the four bridesmaids, dressed in pale yellow. Alison, Hugh's sister, Cecilia, and a local friend were the others. The party that evening was at the Savoy, followed by the Milroy. I did not enjoy myself. Alison paired with the best man, 'Sam' Weller, and I was left with a pompous bore called Peter Sedgeley. The Milroy, in my mind, was the haunt of Peter Dallas Ross, and I had no desire to be amorous.

It was the end of an era. Margaret and I had been very happy in our year together. After their honeymoon, she and Hugh set up house in Cambridge, where he was still an undergraduate.

Once more, my mother and I had begun to irritate each other and I felt it was time to live in London. Two days after the wedding I started a month's cooking course at the Good Housekeeping Institute. It was called a 'Bride's Course', which I felt was a misnomer.

The marriage of Margaret to Captain Hugh Longbourne Browne, RE 3 September 1949. From left to right: Jill McNaughton; Alison McNaughton; Captain 'Sam' Weller; the bride and groom; Cecilia Browne; Jean Norman.

Winsome had found me a room in her digs – 3 Gordon Place, W8, just off Kensington Church Street – and I moved there on 11 September. Two friends of hers were already installed, Jessica Horniman (for whom Peter Wagstaff had fallen) and Tricia Meredith, who was the Assistant Personnel Manager at Harrods. I liked her immediately.[19]

The search for a job went on, and again my quest was literary.

* * *

Publishers' offices in those days were like gentlemen's clubs where books were well-loved friends, rather than the commercial objects they are today. I decided to write to half-a-dozen houses whose typefaces I admired. As far as I remember, they included Collins, Constable, Dennis Dobson, Jonathan Cape, Rupert Hart-Davis (whose *Elephant Bill* by J H Williams I had just devoured) and Chatto and Windus. The last named invited me for an interview.

The offices were in an old house in William IV Street, off St Martin's Lane. Climbing the narrow staircase, I passed a smoke-filled cubby hole where sat a man with a ravaged face and orange fingernails. This was the forty-five year old Cecil Day-Lewis, their reader and one of the directors, later to be Poet Laureate. He was, at that time, the lover of the novelist Rosamond Lehmann, and their steamy affair provided much gossip. Later, his liaison with Elizabeth Jane Howard, another Chatto reader, shocked friends of his wife, the actress Jill Balcon. His raddled eyes appraised me as I mounted the stairs, followed by the stale smell of tobacco.

I was interviewed by Harold Raymond, the Chairman, a kindly, silver-haired man, who offered me a job as secretary to Ian Parsons, one of the partners. Fortunately he suggested a fortnight's trial. As my boss was on holiday, I was to work for the female partner, Norah Smallwood, who was renowned in the publishing world as a virago. Now forty years old, she had started life in the firm as a secretary. Red-haired, hot-tempered and foul-mouthed, she had reduced many secretaries to tears. When Ian, who had been her lover, returned from holiday, yells of 'Ian, you bloody fool' rang through the office. Nor did I take to my boss, whom I described as 'odious, sexy and fat'. His last secretary had left with a nervous breakdown. I shared an office with Ursula Winant, Norah's secretary, whose father John had just become the American Ambassador to Britain. She and I became great friends, and I later attended the engagement party of her sister, Valerie, to Philip Goodhart, reputed, as an undergraduate to have 'the longest tongue in Cambridge';[20] they lived in a pretty house in Edwardes Square, off Kensington High Street.

At the end of the fortnight's trial, the stress and tension, and the sound of Norah yelling at Ian, wore me out and I resigned. (Diana Athill, the celebrated writer, told me recently: 'I never really met the dreaded Norah until she became, for a while, my publisher, in which role she minded her ps and qs – but a cousin once worked as her secretary (very briefly, and no wonder, since she had tried to get away with having no shorthand!) and oh! the tales of tension and terror.') With hindsight, I should have persevered, for the firm had a fine reputation, publishing books of high literary quality. Its authors included Iris Murdoch, Elizabeth Taylor and Aldous Huxley. Two years earlier, they had taken over the Hogarth Press, the small firm founded by Leonard and Virginia Woolf, which had such writers as Vita Sackville West, E M Forster and T S Eliot on its list. Once again, I was out of work.

Life was enlivened by a weekend in Cambridge with Margaret and Hugh, who were 'divinely happy'. Jinny, who had remained in Cambridge, running her successful dancing school, and I went to King's chapel for Matins.

Since the end of her affair with 'K', my mother had been without a man. This autumn she became involved with Frank Saunders, the rich businessman who had lent his

Margaret and Hugh Browne, just married, at a Cambridge dance.

house for Stella's dance and mine and whose wife had recently died of cancer. I do not know how serious their affair was, but I would guess that it was physical. His wealth and affability now that he was alone meant that many of the single local women were angling for his affections. My mother's chief rival was another widow, Elizabeth Valleley, who also lived in Englefield Green. Some months later, to my mother's fury, Frank married her.

* * *

'Universal Aunts' was an upmarket employment agency much used by girls like me who were seeking jobs as secretaries, employers looking for nannies and mother's helps, and parents whose children needed escorting across London.[21] It was from their Sloane Street office that I was sent one day at the end of September to a fine house in Lowndes Square, recently taken over as headquarters of the newly formed 'Lord Mayor's National Thanksgiving Fund'. This somewhat spurious organisation had been hastily formed to raise funds for 'London House', a residential postgraduate college for overseas students in Mecklenburgh Square, near the site of the former Foundling Hospital. The peg on which they hoped to hang their appeal was for people to say 'thank you' to friends overseas for all the food parcels sent across the Atlantic during the war. The fact that many families had received no parcel, and in some cases had never heard of them, was overlooked.

Michael Harvard, the Organising Secretary, was a delightful man of about forty – tall, greying at the temples and stunningly good-looking. His wife had died tragically in a riding accident ten years earlier after only two months of marriage. He was great fun to work for, and I could not have been happier, except that the job was only expected to last for ten months or so. The office was in charge of an office crone called Miss Sayer, a dried-up Australian spinster with no sense of humour. She spent her time issuing directives saying that there would be no smoking or eating of sweets in the office. At first, she and her assistant, Anne Collett, were the only two, apart from me and I found them both trying. Neither had any social life and worked until all hours of the evening, which

I was not prepared to do. As the Fund gained momentum, and more staff arrived, it became more fun. We sent out appeal letters to the Great and the Good in the City, and Debrett became our Bible. Princess Elizabeth was our Patron, and there was constant correspondence between Michael Harvard and HRH's Comptroller at Clarence House, the Hon. Martin Charteris. There was also much to-ing and fro-ing between Lowndes Square and the City, and I was frequently sent down to Mansion House by taxi with urgent letters. It was all rather fun.

Although things seemed smooth enough on the surface, and Michael and I were a good team, I did not know that a power struggle was simmering. One day towards Christmas, I came into work to find that a coup d'état had occurred. Out went the languid and elegant Michael Harvard and in his place was a brisk retired soldier, Brigadier Pepper, known universally as 'Peter', with the air and authority of a 'Captain Mainwaring' of *Dad's Army* fame. Suddenly, the whole ethos of the place changed, and I described it as 'charged with lethargy'. None of us was sure that we liked it.

The year ended with Christmas at home and Midnight Mass at which 'the whole Dallas Ross family' was present. I hardly recognised Peggy: 'Marriage has rounded her so much and now she is much softer, plumper and prettier altogether.... He is as good looking as ever and she obviously adores him.' They invited us to spend Christmas evening with them. Peter was 'very sweet... and I think he has forgiven me for all that is past, for I have treated him despicably.'

* * *

As 1950 progressed, the momentum of The Lord Mayor's National Thanksgiving Fund gathered pace towards the grand inaugural banquet at the Mansion House on 22 March. The atmosphere under the military control of Brigadier Pepper was very different from that of the laid-back Michael Harvard. More staff were taken on, and one of these was a new administrator. Mr Barker was a small, humourless man with an Adolf Hitler moustache who looked like Clement Attlee. It was my misfortune to have to work for him. The dislike was mutual. I christened him 'Clem', but as our relationship soured he became known by all the office as 'the Slug'. One day he and I had a stand-up row and he accused me of 'not pulling my weight'. This infuriated me as I knew I was efficient, and I appealed to the Brigadier. The next day I was transferred to the office of Sir Eric Machtig, a retired colonial civil servant who had been recruited to write the Lord Mayor's speeches. Although he was a boring, pompous individual who tended to treat me like a piece of furniture, he had good hand-writing.

Among the new secretaries was an amusing girl called Diana Barnwell, and I found she knew my cousin, John Hawkesworth. She and I had a lot of fun together. We used to sit on the top of the 74 bus jabbering away in broken English. As it passed St George's Hospital, or some other well-known building, we would say to each other in broken Hungarian, or whatever language we had chosen for that day, 'Oh look, there's Buckingham Palace.' A point would be scored when someone tapped us on the shoulder, as they frequently did, to point out our mistake. Rather puerile but innocent fun which relieved the tedium. One evening we went to a film in Chelsea and met a friend of Diana's called Nicolette. I did not then know what a large part she would play in my life.

The days grew busier, and the tension increased as the banquet drew nearer. On the day itself, having left work at 4.00, we arrived in the City at 6.00, bathed and changed, to witness this great event from the gallery. The ancient Hall was a blaze of colour – blue hydrangeas, scarlet pikemen and trumpeters, gold plate on the long tables. Everyone who was anyone had been invited, and I noted that 'I have never seen so many famous people at such close quarters... Princess Elizabeth looking lovely, the Duchess of Kent (Marina) beautiful, but bored. Churchill also bored stiff, Mrs Churchill regal in white.'

Afterwards, there was a feeling of anti-climax. Press reaction was not all favourable. There was much criticism over the aims and ideals of the Fund. Many people, particularly in the provinces, asked why the memorial should be in London, and 'what is a food parcel?' It was clearly a put-up job. However, a large sum was raised, and the overseas students' hall was established.[22]

After work, music was a great solace and I went to many concerts. I also joined a choir where we sang Brahms' *German Requiem* and Parry's *Blest Pair of Sirens*. My love life was at a low ebb. Miche was so near, physically, whenever I went home, but unattainable. Apart from our fling in Oxford, I knew I meant nothing to him. He and his parents often came over for an evening of bridge, but they would not have welcomed me as a daughter-in-law, for they disliked my mother. A procession of different girl-friends greeted me at weekends. Once or twice he took me out to dinner in London, but our relationship was lukewarm, at least on his side. People in Englefield Green were friendly, but my mother was not popular and I found it embarrassing to be asked to parties on my own.

For the previous few months, my mother had had a job as secretary of the Sunningdale Ladies' Golf Club. She enjoyed this, for it got her out of the house, earned her a bit of money, and she met some interesting people. However, she managed to irritate some of the Committee and one day in June told me that she had been sacked. She decided to give up the lease of Old House Cottage, which she rented unfurnished (in cash) from Miche's parents, and replied to an advertisement in *The Times* for a cook-housekeeper in Essex. It turned out that the family lived at Tye Green, near Stansted,[23] farmed in quite a big way, and kept several horses, complete with girl groom.

At first, all went well. Never a brilliant cook, or very interested in cooking, she nevertheless took herself off for some cooking lessons. She liked Mrs Patten, who said I could go for a weekend whenever I liked. Before dinner, my mother and I would be brought drinks in the kitchen, which I found patronising. However, it was not long before things began to go downhill. Having no home, I used to go down to Essex most weekends. One day, my mother told me that Mrs Patten had decreed that I should visit only once a month. Shortly afterwards, Mrs Patten took me aside and told me that my mother was hopeless as a cook (which did not surprise me, she was hardly cut out for it), and that she would have to go.

* * *

One hot July day, soberly dressed in a navy linen suit and white cloche hat befitting the occasion, I climbed the steep hill towards Hampstead Heath. Near the top, I rang the bell of Upper Terrace House, a handsome Queen Anne edifice set behind a high wall and considered to be 'one of the grandest addresses in London'.[24] The butler who opened the door ushered me into a large drawing-room dominated by Renoir's *Baigneuse blonde* on the chimneypiece. Knowing that my job at the Fund was winding down, I had answered a *Times* advertisement from Sir Kenneth Clark, who needed a secretary. A lion in the art world, he had travelled far from the family cotton mills in Paisley.[25] Now forty-seven years old, urbane, feline and the youngest-ever director of the National Gallery, Sir Kenneth had every reason to be pleased with himself.[26] He sashayed across the room in the extraordinary hip-swinging walk inherited by his son Alan. His tone was unctuous and his voice mellifluous. After looking me up and down, he glanced at my CV. Not having done my homework (the interview had been arranged at short notice), I did not realise that his first question was loaded. 'I see that you were at Cheltenham Ladies' College,' he purred, 'Did you like it?' I replied, with fervour, that I had loathed every minute. 'I'm sorry to hear that – my daughter, Colette, is Senior Prefect and *I* am Chairman of the Governors.' I did not get the job. Perhaps it was as well – I could have been seduced by his handsome son Alan, then aged twenty-one. Kenneth Clark and his wife were not popular with their peers – he was considered effete and she had a drink problem.[27]

Sir Kenneth Clark, art historian, to whom I applied unsuccessfully (to my later relief!) for the post of secretary.

I hoped that my job with the Fund would continue until the spring. It was therefore a shock to be told by the Brigadier in November that my contract would finish at the end of December. Homeless, jobless, rootless – once again.

Nor was there room at the inn for Christmas until Tricia Meredith suggested that we should join them at Aldeburgh where she and her family had stayed for many years. The Uplands was a private house opposite the church which belonged to two amusing and enterprising sisters, Connie and Joy Winn. Having been left on their own, without much money, they turned their family home into an elegant hotel, complete with their own butler, cook and family silver. The place was run like a house party, there was no advertising and it was very much 'by invitation only'. The place was full of Etonians: Tricia's stepfather, Michael Impey, her two stepbrothers, Charles[28] and Hugh, Felix Markham, an historian who was Dean of Hertford College, Oxford, and several other dons and hangers-on. It was bliss, there was much teasing and laughter, and we fitted in immediately. My mother loved it as the main evening game was bridge and she was a good player.

When the New Year arrived, we had to make some hard decisions. With our furniture in store, we were both homeless. We decided to find a London flat and live together.

Notes

1 See *Not the Purser's Daughter?*, page 136.

2 This extract from my diary for 25 March 1946 was written when I was twenty. The description of my father starts on the previous page:

> I think it's his hypocrisy that irritates me the most. He must always know more, and be better than anybody else and is continually belittling other people's opinions or else seeming amazed that they should have any. Perhaps that is rather a hard judgement and possibly he does not give that impression to other people, certainly not to the casual stranger, who are all under his spell when he turns on the charm, but he has given Mummy such an inferiority complex and done her so much mental harm that I can never forgive him. On the other hard, no-one is all bad and there is doubtless a great deal of good in him, if one could plumb the depths. Jaa [my sister Peggy, who died in 1940; see volume 2 (p.83) of these memoirs, *Not the Purser's Daughter?*], I think was the one person who could do this and was the one person he really loved. I know what a loss it was to him when she went away and he feels it still and although I do my best to take her place and be interested in the things that she was, I am well aware that in his eyes I am half her worth and it is an observation that is not conducive to a deep affection.
>
> Darling little Jaa, how I miss you. Oh! What fun we could all have had together, were we not a divided family, both by death and circumstance. I often wonder whether perhaps the fact of having no Family – only my little Mung [my mother], and no home life, has not perhaps had some effect on me psychologically. Contributed in some way to the deep inferiority complex, from which, in some ways, I still suffer. The feeling I am different from other people in not having an absorbing family life. I know it is in a great measure due to the fact that we are not well off, and I know I feel inferior to these society girls who seem to have everything in life, money, breeding, looks and a good time. As I write that, I realise, but how foolish, my child. These are not the things which matter in life – is not the deep and abiding Love of a Mother worth all the gold in the world? Is not the realisation and appreciation of the worthwhile things in life more important than the superficial and artificial?...

3 Hugh Browne and Tony Landale. Each would marry one of my cousins.

4 Peter Dallas Ross and I hardly knew each other. Fifty-four years later I would discover his deep love of music and art. See pages 143–7.

5 See page 50.

6 Rather pious and pompous.

7 'The chosen of my heart'.

8 See *Call Back Yesterday*, volume 1 of my memoirs, page 89.

9 Described by Julian Critchley in *A Bag of Boiled Sweets* as 'a dull industrial chemist'. He was knighted in 1986.

10 He went on to a distinguished career as a scientist: Nobel Prizewinner, OM, FRS, and created Lord Porter of Luddington in 1990 (1920–2002).

[11] See *Not the Purser's Daughter?*, page 38.

[12] She was killed in an air crash the following year.

[13] At that time, she was fifty-four years old.

[14] He later became Bishop of Guildford (1962) and of Salisbury (1973). My godson is now Lieutenant General Sir Alistair Irwin KCB CBE Colonel of the Black Watch (RHR) from 2003 until the Regiment became part of the Royal Regiment of Scotland in 2006. He is now Chairman of the Black Watch Regimental Trust.

[15] See *Not the Purser's Daughter?*, page 120.

[16] So good, in fact, that I've remembered it, word for word, for over sixty years.

[17] The author of *Anatomy of Britain* and many other well-known books.

[18] Introduced to me by George Reindorp and which we used at our own wedding.

[19] She later married Ronnie Sedgwick, a delightful man with an infectious sense of humour.

[20] Conservative MP for Beckenham 1957–92 and briefly a junior minister.

[21] They are still going strong and their motto 'Anything for anyone at any time' still holds.

[22] Then known as 'London House', now 'Goodenough College'. It is in Mecklenburgh Square.

[23] Probably now gobbled up by the airport

[24] Anthony Blond, *Jew Made in England*, Timewell Press, 2004.

[25] Coats and Clark thread

[26] Appointed at the early age of thirty-one.

[27] *The Diaries of Cynthia Gladwyn*, edited by Miles Jebb, Constable, 1995.

[28] Later an Eton housemaster.

The marriage of Alison McNaughton to Captain Anthony Landale, RE at Stansted parish church, April 1951.

Chapter 4

Deliverance

'One foot in sea and one on shore,
To one thing constant never'

Much Ado About Nothing 2.3.67–68

After weeks of searching from Hampstead to Hammersmith, my mother told me early in January 1951 that she had found somewhere to live. Although we had hoped to find something unfurnished, so that we could take our furniture out of store, there was nothing that we could afford.

Number 14 Welbeck Mansions, Addison Bridge Road, was a furnished flat near Olympia. It lay in a cul-de-sac overlooking the busy Earl's Court to Olympia railway. It had three small bedrooms and a sitting-room and was furnished in a curiously old-fashioned style. My mother paid six and a half guineas a week, the most she could afford. The owner, Mark Tennyson-d'Eyncourt, seemed reasonable and we prepared to make the best of it.

While I had been homeless, Nancy and my father had offered me a room in their flat near Regent's Park. (My mother was living in an Earls Court hotel.) From here, I made frequent forays into central London trying to find a job. Each one I thought possible Nancy vetoed as 'quite unsuitable'– my father took little interest.

My stepmother, an intelligent woman, felt I was too 'airy-fairy'; that I should abandon my literary pretensions and concentrate instead on finding a well paid, stable job in commerce. She probably had a point.

Nancy and I had a difficult relationship at first. Loud-voiced and strident, she had a sharp tongue and at the age of twenty-five I resented her very personal remarks which she delivered without hesitation or thought for my feelings. Thick-skinned herself,

I don't think she had any idea she was giving offence. It was just the way she spoke – staccato rasps that came out unthinkingly. It was not until I married a strong man who stood up to her that our relationship improved. She had a deep sense of family and would be a most generous step-grandmother.

Although I found her scatological humour unattractive and their way of life, with its endless pub crawling, unappealing, my father adored her. A weak man, he liked being bossed[1] – and it was a comfort to me that he was now looked after and did not rely on me as a constant crutch.

The job hunting continued until eventually, after endless interviews, I accepted one at the BBC as secretary to the Assistant Head of Audience Research.

Everyone was known by their initials. My boss was 'AHAR' and the head of department 'HAR'. Although I did not know it at the time, Audience Research was a backwater in the Corporation's vast empire. My boss, Mr Littman, was pleasant enough – a Lithuanian Jew whose family had arrived in this country before the war – but the job was dull. Audience Research employed volunteers up and down the country to report on the various programmes. (This was mainly radio – television was in its infancy.) Keen listeners could write in and offer their time. They were mainly old ladies or people who were otherwise housebound, and they filled in a long form listing their various comments.

Two weeks later, one of my job-hunting letters came home to roost. Before Christmas, I had written to half-a dozen publishers, as books and publishing were my *raison d'être*. Now, having started at the BBC, I heard from a new firm, Dennis Dobson Ltd, asking me to go for an interview. (I can't imagine why I chose them – they were not well-known and specialised in music. I can only think that my interest had been sparked by working in the music department of Heffers.) My immediate reaction was to refuse, but my mother persuaded me that one had to go for things in this life. The next day, in my lunch hour, I dashed down to St James' Place and after a short chat with Dennis Dobson and his major-domo, James Gordon, agreed to start in April. The job would cover everything from tea-making to editing. I felt this was the start in publishing which I was seeking. I returned to the BBC where my boss received the news with equanimity. His only comment – a fair one – was that he hoped Dobson was solvent.

Looking back, I am amazed at the speed with which I picked up and put down jobs, and it was hardly surprising that I failed to settle anywhere. Perhaps it was the peripatetic nature of my life, the instability of my home and the agony of being unloved, but I must have been a most difficult employee. If only, if only I had kept up my Latin and gone to Oxford, then I would have had some purpose in life. There was no one to tell me that Oxford and Cambridge were not the only choices – many other excellent universities, such as London, did not require Latin. And so I meandered on.

Early in February, I went up to Cambridge to stay with Jinny. She had moved from Chesterton Road and was now living, with several others, in Scrope Terrace, near the Fitzwilliam. She was still teaching dancing, and also working as secretary to Kenneth Pickthorn, the MP for Cambridge University, to make ends meet, but, like me, was 'in a miasma about her future'. Her engagement to Bob Fraser-Mackenzie, a Scottish laird, had been broken off the previous year. Anthony Lowe, a Queens' College alumnus whom she had taught to dance, was in the United States on a postgraduate scholarship, but they kept in touch.

On 9 February, I had an unpleasant lunch with my father. A few weeks earlier, my cousin Beryl had been married in Finchley. My father had been invited with both Nancy and my mother. Apparently, flushed with champagne, my mother had said that, in the eyes of the Church, both she and Nancy were scarlet women. It was meant to be a joke. Everyone laughed except my father, who was incensed. He had no sense of humour. Neither he nor Nancy, he declared, would accept our joint invitations until they received an apology. It was typical of him that, instead of tackling her head-on, he used me as a football.

Since my confirmation in Cambridge, I had become deeply religious and attended both Holy Trinity, Brompton (where the padre was the delightful Pat Gilliat), and St Stephen's, Rochester Row.

Here, the High Anglican rite of confession gave me peace from my many demons. I felt dissatisfied with my life and turned to God in an effort to improve it. I also resolved to be kinder to my mother.

George Reindorp, the vicar of St Stephen's, whom I had met at Alistair Irwin's christening, was both inspiring and charismatic. His powerful sermons attracted a large congregation which included many females, especially the nurses from St Thomas' Hospital. I now decided to join the Quest Club, a group which met regularly on weekday evenings. I also became a member of the 'Church Watching' team, single people who volunteered to sit alone in two-hour stints at the back of the church to watch for thieves and other marauders. There was no sense, in those days, that this might be a dangerous task for a lone young woman but the district of Victoria held fewer drunks and druggies than it does today.

Apart from Miche, there was no man in my life. He continued to take me out now and then, but there was no warmth in our relationship, which was perfunctory and sterile. I resisted, just, the temptation to fall in love.

Despite the dullness of the BBC, I made some good friends. One of these was Awdry May, a cousin of the Reverend W. Awdry, creator of Thomas the Tank Engine. Now thirty-four and an executive, she had been with 'the Corp' for twelve years and had started as a secretary. She told me that Audience Research was a 'dead-end' department and I felt justified in leaving it. She, like me, loved the theatre and together we saw some memorable productions: Laurence Olivier and Vivien Leigh appearing together in a double season of Shaw's *Caesar and Cleopatra* and Shakespeare's *Antony and Cleopatra* at the St James's Theatre, now demolished. Their performances were spellbinding.

This was the year of the Festival of Britain, commemorating the centenary of Prince Albert's Great Exhibition in 1851. (The Festival was the brainchild of the senior Labour politician Herbert Morrison, who felt that people needed a tonic.) After six years of peace, the country was beginning to shake off the shades of rationing and austerity – everyone wanted to celebrate. There was still much wartime bomb damage and London needed rebuilding. The south bank of the Thames came alive for the Festival, and the new Festival Hall was opened as a venue for classical music.

London was full of music which continued to give me solace in my loneliness. I started a record collection. The new 12-inch long-playing records had just come out. At nine shillings and eight pence each, they were not cheap. (Before their advent, it was necessary to play four or six 78s to hear a whole symphony, turning each record over every five minutes.) I bought Mozart's 40th Symphony and J S Bach's Double Concerto in D minor for two violins, played by Yehudi Menuhin and George Enescu.

Although my mother was still my closest friend, we continued to irritate each other living at such close quarters. We found the flat claustrophobic, dark and noisy. It was difficult to sleep above the railway. We were both spinning in a maelstrom of self-doubt. At the end of March, her brother-in-law, Will Shiell, suggested that she should take a job as companion to a paralysed friend of his, a Mrs Fox, who lived near Harpenden. As we were so out of harmony with each other and I missed my independence, we decided to part company. Prices of flats had leapt up since January, owing to the forthcoming Festival of Britain. However, to my surprise, I found an unfurnished room with bathroom in Linden Gardens, Notting Hill for only £2 a week. (Notting Hill was a grotty enclave then, not the fashionable district it now is.) I saw the room at night, and it was not until I moved in that I realised there was no outlook except a brick wall. The room was tiny, and there was just room for a bed, a dressing-table and a chair. I cooked on a gas ring in the bathroom. However, it was good to have some of my own things around me, and I decided to make the best of it.

Ever since they met in the Cambridge flat my double cousin Margaret and I had shared in 1949, her sister Alison and Tony Landale had been going out together. Tony was Hugh Browne's best friend and, like him, a Sapper. He had been doing an Army engineering degree but at St Catharine's rather than Trinity Hall. A countryman with a good sense of humour, he adored dogs and was one of the few people I know who could recognise birdsong. They were married at Stansted Parish Church on 21 April. Although I was not a bridesmaid, I was asked to the party at the Berkeley afterwards. It was fun. Margaret and Hugh missed the wedding, as Hugh had been appointed to the British Military Mission to Burma and they were living in Rangoon. Shortly after their marriage, Tony and Alison sailed for Cyprus as his unit had been posted to Nicosia.

Early in April I had said farewell to the BBC and started my new job. Dennis Dobson's offices were at the top of an eighteenth-century house off St James' Street. It was a small concern consisting of Dobson, James Gordon, Henry, a production manager, a reader called 'Mac', another secretary and me. Dobson was a tall, gangly young man of about thirty-four, very musical, who had started the firm four years earlier. He was hopelessly impractical and all the office clocks were kept half-an-hour fast as he had no idea of time. The brains and engine power of the business came from Gordon, a small, rotund Cockney with a round face, a crimped and wavy crew cut. When I had seen them in February, I thought that Gordon and Dobson might be a couple of gays (or pansies, as we called them in those days). I was wrong. Gordon was a rabid communist. He did not take to me. Dobson, he and I sat in one small room. When I answered the telephone, he mimicked my voice in a la-di-da fashion. I ignored him, but should have retaliated by talking Cockney. They mainly published books on music and did not appear to be making money.

On 10 May, Miche announced his engagement to Mary Campbell Penney, a major-general's daughter. This explained his coolness during the early spring.[2]

My mother had taken the Harpenden job and I visited her often. I felt rootless without a home. Mrs Fox was a kind woman of about forty-eight who said I could go down whenever I liked. She was badly paralysed and needed constant attention. Unfortunately she had no sense of humour, and my mother found the life very dull.

Sundays in London were lonely. One day I bumped into Jinny's ex-dancing pupil, Anthony Lowe, who was just back from America. After Cambridge he had won an English Speaking Union scholarship to the University of Minnesota where he gained an MSc in agricultural engineering. He was now in London, working for Monsanto, the American chemical firm, and living nearby in Ladbroke Grove.

I asked him round for a drink. He told me, years later, that he was appalled at the size of my room, 'like a sardine tin', and thought it very dark and depressing. There was no view, only a slit of sky, out of the stained-glass window. It was nice having him round the corner and I saw him quite often. One evening he took me to the Fun Fair at Battersea and we went on the Ghost Train together. He and Jinny were still pirouetting round each other, but were not, as yet, 'an item'.

My loneliness and spiritual desolation increased, and I prayed for deliverance from a life which seemed to have no roots, no purpose and no future. On 28 June, the other secretary and I were told that Dobson's was in a parlous state financially, and that we should look round for something else. On the same day, I had a letter from Margaret asking me to go out to Burma in September and spend six months with them. She had been worrying about me because I had sounded 'so sad' in my last letter. My prayer had been answered in the most amazing way.

The invitation was not without problems. My stepmother did not approve. She thought, rightly, that I was far too much of a flibbertigibbet and that it was high time I settled down. My father, surprisingly, was in favour. He thought that experience of life and travel is never wasted and that I should go. Then there was the cost. I had no money of my own, and the little I earned went on keep. My mother was very supportive and generously offered to pay the fare of £300. In those days, flights to Burma did not exist – the reality was a five-week voyage. There were two shipping lines, Bibby, which was up-market, and Henderson, the opposite. There was no question of Bibby. It was much too expensive and in any case they were fully booked.

On 12 July, I had a cable: 'Annabel Mary Browne was born at 3.5 a.m. this morning. She has dark hair, eyes, perfect skin. Is beautiful.' I was asked to be one of her godmothers.

My mother was getting very bored with Mrs Fox. She had a

little capital of her own and decided to build a house at Englefield Green. Her brother-in-law, Stewart, was horrified and thought it a most foolhardy enterprise. It was a wise decision – it gave her an interest while I was away, and she was tough enough to continue against stiff family opposition. It cost £3,000 and proved to be an excellent investment.[3] My flat was proving difficult to let. Although I had seventy-nine replies from an advertisement in the *Evening Standard,* only four were possible. When people arrived, they were appalled how small it was, and I cursed myself that I had not made this clear. Eventually, after 216 replies in all, I let it to a charming female doctor.

I left Dobson's for good on 7 September. 'I don't know when I have hated a job so much ... the last five months have been the most disagreeable in my whole life.' On Friday 21 September I sailed in SS *Salween* for Burma.

It was a journey that would change my life.

Notes

[1] Rather like the Duke of Windsor.
[2] I did not see him again for years, but in 1968 he and his wife came to a drinks party we gave in London.
[3] Today in 2010, it is worth nearly one million pounds.

Chapter 5

Burma

'By indirections, find directions out'

Hamlet 2.1.66

The familiar skyline of Liverpool faded into the distance as we edged into the Irish Sea. SS *Salween* was tiny, smaller than a cross-channel ferry. Henderson Line was, as I have said, much inferior to Bibby. It was a freight line that carried a few passengers. Most were Burmese returning home after leave. The handful of British were mainly the wives of port officials and minor civil servants. Apart from Gladys, a Maltese girl travelling to Port Said, I was the only unattached female on board. The crew were Indian, Burmese and Lascar, most of whom called me 'Miss Sahib'. I found it difficult to get used to shouting 'Boy!' in the approved European manner, which seemed to be expected.

I shared a cabin with Thelma Marjoribanks, a pleasant woman who was travelling to Port Sudan. Although it was still summer, the nights were cold and we wore overcoats on deck. After two days at sea, we reached the Bay of Biscay and the ship began to roll. The night of 24 September was very rough. Few people slept and most were tossed from side to side. I only stayed in my top bunk by hanging on to the sides with both hands. The wind howled, a gale warning was put out, and nothing on board was safe unless it was securely lashed. Doors banged and crockery crashed to the deck. Seasoned travellers said it was one of the worst nights they could remember. There was a huge sea next day but, to my surprise, I did not feel ill and was one of the few people who turned up for every meal. The food was excellent, usually four or five courses. Having nothing to do except lie about on deck reading or chatting, I began to put on weight. Because of the languid and soporific nature of this form of travel, most people turned in at about 8.30pm.

Once we had passed Cape Finisterre and Gibraltar, the weather became warmer. The ship began to come to life. Summer dresses came out and deck games were organised. Sometimes we danced in the evening to gramophone records with the ship's officers, young men in their early twenties from Liverpool and Glasgow. Some of them were excellent dancers. Although the people were unexciting, they were all pleasant. The only kindred spirit on board was the doctor, Nigel Sparrow, a chap in his fifties who turned out to be the brother of Jinny's huntin', shootin' and fishin' friends with whom we had stayed on Dartmoor during our hitch-hiking tour. He was great fun, and each of us was glad to have the company of the other.

As we approached the North African coast, the huge mountainous mass of Morocco, dark and mysterious, rose on the skyline. The sea was an incredible blue. Nearing Port Said, the heat increased. Awnings were put up on deck and every fan and blower turned on. Now the sea changed from bright blue to the deep olive green of the Nile. I realised why it is called eau-de-Nil.

On the afternoon of 2 October, we docked in Port Said. At once the ship was surrounded by dozens of small craft, ancient sailing-boats, canoes and feluccas. Hordes of Egyptian traders in scarlet fezzes manoeuvred their boats alongside, climbing the masts until they were level with the lower deck of the ship and could dangle their wares under our noses. Some, more enterprising than the rest, swarmed up the side on rope ladders, leaping nimbly on to the deck in order to catch a likely customer before their competitors.

'Hullo there, Miss Queen Mary, lovely handbags, real crocodile,' one would shout, while another tried with 'Come on, Mrs. Simpson, buy a genuine Turkish carpet, only £2.' Exotically coloured carpets showing scenes of the Sphinx and the Pyramids, or Egyptian dancing girls, were going for thirty shillings. Sunhats in red, blue and green could be bought, after some tough bargaining, for as little as half a crown. Real leather suitcases at £2 each, brief cases, ivory camels, coloured necklaces, musical boxes, bananas and melons were laid out in the boats. Most of it was junk. Any likely looking men were waylaid with a leer – 'feelthy postcards, very feelthy indeed'.

Then there was the *gully-gully* man, a greasy Egyptian conjuror with padded shoulders and permed hair, who delighted the children by producing day-old chicks from their noses and ears. Later, when it was cooler, we went ashore. Everything seemed to be a dirty, dusty, yellowy brown. The odour of stale sweat and the stench of sewage pervaded. I mounted a camel and had my photograph taken.

The following day we left Port Said and proceeded slowly down the Suez Canal. Built by the French engineer, Ferdinand de Lesseps in 1869 to join the Mediterranean and the Red Sea, it is a marvellous piece of engineering. Formerly ships had to travel round the Cape of Good Hope, but now they could enjoy a much shorter route. I found its 119 miles of sand, camels and palm trees a monotonous journey. Now and then we saw a team of Arab workmen doing repair work at the side of the canal or sailing feluccas that had changed little since biblical times. That night we stopped for several hours in the Bitter Lakes (the salt-water lakes that divide the northern and southern parts of the Canal) to allow a convoy to pass. Next day, we arrived in Suez and were almost in the Red Sea. It was beginning to get unbearably hot.

Friday 5 October and into the Red Sea with a vengeance. It was so hot at night that we slept, or tried to, with ventilators up, all the fans going and cabin doors open, and we even dispensed with the covering of a sheet. It was much cooler on deck where there was the chance of a breeze. Gladys, the Maltese girl, had disembarked at Port Said, and I was the only single female on board. There was no chance of a flirtation – the ship's officers were all far too young and unsophisticated. Only the Burmese ambassador, an attractive man of 35, gave me the glad eye.

The next day we docked at Port Sudan where we were due to stay for five days while we unloaded cargo. Thelma Marjoribanks, my cabinmate, now left us to travel to Khartoum. The Sudanese porters were tall, attractive, muscular men with high cheekbones and strong, glistening bodies that shone in the sunlight like polished conkers. As they moved the heavy pieces of freight, they chanted weird tribal songs. Sometimes a brown grinning face would appear in the cabin window, framed in a mass of coarse, rug-like woolly hair, frizzed at the ends in mutton fat. When the vision, after much rolling of the eyes, eventually disappeared, a faint odour of stale body and curry powder hung in the air. Some of the passengers called them 'fuzzy wuzzies' – a term that would horrify people today. One was taller and more handsome than the rest; Dr Sparrow, a talented artist, drew him for me. Unloading the cargo continued all night, and as mine was a forward cabin there was little sleep. During the day, the heat was almost unbearable, reaching about 108 degrees Fahrenheit, 45 Centigrade. Hardened travellers laughed and said that this was nothing – we should have been here in July! I felt quite faint and sick. One of the Burmese passengers collapsed with sunstroke. There was nothing to do except lie on one's bed and expire with heat.

Five days later we sailed. It was blessedly cool at sea after the inferno of Port Sudan. Having offloaded two thousand tons of cargo, the ship rolled ominously, and there was nothing to do after dinner, except go to bed. Thankfully I was for'ard, which was much cooler. After two days, we arrived in Aden, where we were to offload another two thousand tons. We sailed into the harbour at night – a sight of breathtaking beauty. The town is built on the side of a huge, dark mountain. A thousand lights, red, blue, white and green, twinkled in the darkness. There was a full moon and one bright star hovered in the sky. By the time we had docked, it was almost too late to go ashore. However, we did so, to find that most of the shops had closed. The smell of the town was indescribable – drains, body odour and curry, the scent of the Middle East that will be with me for ever. Next morning we sailed again, and passed six days at sea until we reached Colombo on 20 October.

News from home filtered through the ship's wireless. King George VI was not well. His health had been poor throughout the summer. It was announced he had flu, but in late September he was operated on at Buckingham Palace. Although the anxiety was played down, it was clear that he was an ill man. No specific cause was given, but it was rumoured that he had arterial problems in his legs.[1] Princess Elizabeth and Prince Philip would go to Australia in January in his stead.

World news was also worrying. There was tension in the East. Liaquat Ali Khan, the first Prime Minister of the newly created Pakistan had been assassinated. There were skirmishes between our troops and the Egyptians in Ismailia. A British soldier had been murdered, and half a million pounds worth of damage was done in the subsequent rioting. The Egyptians had fired on a convoy of lorries crossing the Suez Canal. The Parachute Regiment, my cousin Tony Landale among them, was ordered from Cyprus to help the East Lancashire Regiment quell the disturbances.

In Colombo, a town of great beauty, I had been given an introduction to some friends of the Brownes, and boldly took a taxi on my own. I had lunch in their bungalow overlooking the sea.

Now we were on the last lap: only five more days until we docked in Rangoon. The voyage had been fascinating, but some of the passengers were backbiters. I found the endless malicious gossiping of people who had nothing better to do very trying.

On Wednesday 24 October, the ship lay in the Gulf of Martaban, waiting for the tide to take us into the Irrawaddy Delta and Rangoon. The following morning I woke at a quarter to seven to find we were anchored in the estuary, just outside the city. In the early morning sunlight the massive golden globe of the Shwe Dagon pagoda shimmered in the distance. It was not until noon that we tied up. Among the many people furiously waving on the dockside were Hugh and Margaret. My voyage had ended at last – a momentous six months lay ahead.

* * *

His Majesty's Military Mission to Burma was quite small – two dozen married officers from all three services and a few bachelors, headed by the fifty-five-year-old Major General Bertram Temple. In 1949 General Ne Win, Burma's dictatorial military leader, had refused Britain's invitation to join the Commonwealth and had

The Shwe Dagon pagoda in Rangoon and a golden Buddha at Mandalay.

insisted upon independence.[2] In order to smooth the transition, London authorised loans, arms and the dispatch of a British Services Mission. The married quarters were about six miles north of Rangoon, on the shores of the Great Lake. It was a beautiful place – green trees, little islands, scarlet tropical flowers, bougainvillea, canna, hibiscus – every imaginable colour was there. Hugh and Margaret's bungalow was on the very edge of the lake. Hugh warned me to be careful of snakes – the place was alive with them, and there was a nest of cobras in the woodwork over the front door. I was introduced to my three-month-old goddaughter and pronounced her 'just divine – the most heavenly little thing, far prettier than in her photographs'.

The most pressing need was to get a job, as I did not intend to trespass on the Brownes' hospitality but to pay my way. There seemed to be only one possible job going, for a secretary at the Embassy, but I would have to stay for at least a year. I agonised with my conscience – my mother was expecting me home in May when the house she was building would be finished, and I did not know if I could leave her for so long. Everyone told me that, at twenty-six, I must start thinking about myself and that after so much moving around this might be the start of a serious career. I decided to accept, but would not have confirmation from the Foreign Office in London until mid-November.

Almost at once, I was whisked off into the social life of the Mission. The evening after my arrival, we heard that the Tories had won the general election. A small majority, only seventeen, but everyone was thrilled that six years of Labour rule were over. A celebration party was immediately thrown by Desmond Parkinson, a fair, attractive man who was Second Secretary at the Embassy. I discovered that his wife, Anne, was the sister of Susan Durnford, one of Miche's most favoured girl-friends.

I had been warned on the boat that Rangoon was a veritable 'fishing fleet'. There were few single girls, and those who, like me, had been imported came in for a fair bit of ribbing. Of the dozen or so bachelors, some worked at the Embassy, some for multinationals such as the Hongkong and Shanghai Bank, Steele Brothers (which, among other things, extracted teak from Burmese forests) and Swires, a long-established Far Eastern company with interests in property, aviation and shipping. Others were attached to the Military Mission.

The Parkinsons' party was a magical introduction to Burma. Their bungalow, like the Brownes', lay on the shores of the lake. The lawns, crowded with men in white dinner-jackets and their wives in filmy evening dresses, were in darkness. The only light came from hundreds of coloured fairy lanterns threaded through the trees. Indian servants, in stiff white jackets and pink turbans, handed round drinks. There was a mood of euphoria, with people slapping each other on the back, celebrating a change of government.

Margaret led me through the throng to where a tall, red-headed young man with a ginger moustache was holding court. Charismatic and arrogant, Captain Geoffrey Webb-Bowen, Rifle Brigade, was fully aware that he was devilishly attractive to women.[3] He looked me up and down without interest before turning back to his harem.

The hub of social life for the small British contingent was the

Sailing Club, and I was soon installed as a member. Races on the lake took place every weekend and lone girls like me were much in demand as crew. I was thankful that I had learned to sail with Hilly and Harold Wyllie, so was not a novice.

The place throbbed with sex. Take a group of lusty young men, introduce one or two nubile females, add the heat and mystery of the East, and you have a potent mixture. The main drink was whisky, to which I was unused, and the parties were wild. A few nights after my arrival I became embroiled in one of these boister-ous affairs where the men started to put lumps of ice down the girls' dresses. They also decided to 'christen' me by pouring neat whisky down my throat. In the fracas, my dress got torn to shreds – luckily I was wearing a decent bra. One of the liveliest of the bachelors was a tall young Wykehamist, Mike May Somerville, who was working for Steele Brothers. He was a great tease, would pat my hips (which had become rather large) and christened me 'Harry Hippers'. A couple of weeks later, the fishing fleet was en-larged by the arrival of the Anglican bishop's nieces, Jane and Eliz-abeth Downing, two attractive girls who were immediately dubbed the 'Bee's Knees'. Another newcomer at about this time was the twenty-five-year-old Bill Harding, who had joined Desmond Parkinson's small department in the Embassy. A handsome lothario, he set many hearts a-flutter, but not mine.[4]

Most of the attractive bachelors, like Geoff Webb-Bowen, al-ready had steady girl friends and were therefore bespoke. One who was single was the General's ADC, Captain Richard Sale, Royal Horse Guards. The son of His Majesty's Crown Equerry, he had known Miche at Eton. A month after my arrival, he told Margaret that he was 'desperately in love' with me. She advised patience as I was clearly uninterested. Soon afterwards, he proposed marriage: flattering, but I found him young and immature.

The most beautiful part of the country was in the north, but there was little opportunity to see it as a civil war was raging be-tween the Burmese and the mainly Karen insurgents. Most of the northern states were out-of-bounds to members of the Mission, as General Temple deemed them too dangerous for unattached

Rangoon: the Great
Lake at sunset.

females. The furthest we were allowed to go was to Mandalay and
to Pegu, where there was a huge golden reclining Buddha. I longed
to visit the former princely Shan States where the main industry
was opium-growing. I was told these were wild places with wide
valleys hedged in by rugged mountain ranges.

Rather to my relief, the Embassy job did not materialise. I still
had a raw conscience about my mother and would not have felt
happy about staying away for as long as a year. She had left the
Harpenden job as Mrs Fox had decided to live with her former
housemaid. Searching the columns of the *Lady*, she found a living-
in job as companion to a Mrs Watkins at Shorne in Kent. I felt desperately sorry that she was reduced to this, and my guilt redoubled.
Fortunately her house at Englefield Green was taking shape, and
she hoped to have moved in by April.

I was lucky enough to find a secretarial job with May and Baker,
the pharmaceutical company that had created the drug M&B.
Geoffrey Webb-Bowen warned me that Derek Crookes, the
twenty-nine-year-old local boss, was 'a bit of a wolf'. At least I
would be earning something, and could repay both the Brownes
and my mother for the fare.[5]

Ian Cowan, a businessman who worked for Glaxo, gave me a lift

89

in and out each day. Although Rangoon was only six miles distant, the journey often took up to an hour. Out in the country, on the grass-lined verges and almost swallowed by the encroaching jungle, were small shrines dedicated to Buddha or one of the local gods. As we approached the city, the traffic increased – bullock carts and bicycles wove in and out of the cars. Sometimes an animal would escape, causing fury among the motorists. Large lorry-like buses, crammed to bursting with Burmese, Indian and Chinese, darted round corners on two wheels, scattering the pedestrians. Thin Pi dogs, with every rib protruding and suffering from hideous red mange, slunk out of sight down the alleyways, biting their backs in agony until they were raw and bleeding. They were often knocked down by the traffic and their stinking corpses would rot in the sun until they were devoured by the purple-throated vultures that wheeled menacingly overhead, ready for the kill. Small stalls selling strongly scented curry dishes, vegetables, necklaces or the locally brewed hooch lined the road. Poverty was everywhere. Three or four families might live all together in a rush roofed basha hut, raised from the ground on short wooden stakes, with their goats, cows and dogs.

As we approached the city, our way might be barred by one of the many beggars, asking for alms. Many had ragged, emaciated bodies that contrasted strangely with the well-fed merchants, fat and prosperous in their silk lungis. Some of the beggars might be genuine, but more often they would be small children who had been deliberately mutilated to excite pity. There was one tiny legless boy who managed to move with amazing speed on his rump, using his arms as paddles. I found him almost repulsive, so swift and intimidating was his demand for charity. Amid the traffic, we would sometimes see a fat merchant being pulled along in rickshaw by a sweating coolie. This inhuman form of transport was dying out, and being replaced by the more civilised trishaw in which two passengers sat back to back while a hot and puffing driver pedalled furiously. Once in the city, the smell was overpowering. In all except the main thoroughfares, people relieved themselves casually in the open drains which lined the side streets. Rangoon was a new city – built by the British overlords only a century earlier. Most of the centre was well planned, with wide tree-lined boulevards rather like Paris. The buildings looked modern and European.

On 5 December I had a 'very worrying' letter from my mother. The job with Mrs Watkins was 'no good' and she was again rootless. I was glad I was not staying away for a year – 'I don't think she could bear it.' Once again, Stewart and Enid came to the rescue and asked her for Christmas.

On 6 February 1952 we heard that the King had died peacefully in his sleep at Sandringham. A footman taking in his early morning tea had been unable to wake him. Although we knew he was seriously ill, it was still a shock. He had cancer of the lung, but in those buttoned-up days the dread word was never uttered. Princess Elizabeth, deputising for her father on a state visit to Australia, had reached Kenya. At Treetops Hotel, built in a wild fig tree in the Aberdare National Park, Prince Philip told his wife that she was now Queen. They returned to England at once. All festivities in Burma ceased immediately. Flags on public buildings were flown at half-mast. The Mission observed a week's mourning; officers wore black arm-bands and all parties and sailing races were cancelled. On 15 February, a memorial service for the King was held in Rangoon Cathedral. Representatives from every country, the Diplomatic Corps and the Services and people of all nationalities came to pay homage. The emotional service included the 'Dead March' from Handel's *Saul*, 'Last Post' and 'God Save The Queen', which we sang for the first time. Later, at home, we switched on the wireless and heard the whole of the funeral service broadcast on the World Service from St George's Chapel, Windsor. Even in those days, when radio communication was not sophisticated, the transmission was amazingly clear – so clear, in fact, that we could hear the neighing of the horses, the chink of their bits, and the clatter of hooves on the frosted cobbles.

After the period of mourning was over, the hedonistic life continued. Wild, drunken parties were followed by mellow moonlight picnics on the lake. Sometimes we went out for a meal at a little restaurant, the Nam Sing, up the road. Chinese food – fried chicken, noodles and mushrooms, baked crabs, pan rolls – was a new and delicious experience. One evening the Netherlands Minister organised a beagle hunt. We rushed round Rangoon in teams of four collecting live cockroaches, reading hidden messages under bridges, dashing through drainpipes and finding whisky labels. It was all rather juvenile.

On 7 April, Margaret, Hugh and I gave a party which in some ways was my farewell. We turned the house into a night club called the 'Inferno', symbolising Hell, and people said it was the most roaring success Rangoon had ever known. Hugh made papier mâché lanterns and borrowed a skull from the doctor, in which he put a candle. Then we had a cabaret – Margaret and I sang a song 'We're Two Sexy Sisters of Satan', with words by John Smith, one of the bachelors; Geoffrey dressed up as a woman and did a shadow stunt behind a curtain of taking a bath, and I sang 'I Cain't Say No' from *Oklahoma!* Hugh then distributed prizes for the most enterprising devil, for which I wrote the script (which I still have). It was rather witty, but by this time everyone had had so much to drink, having come on from another party, and there was so much noise that most of my words were lost. There was a great deal of flirting behind the cannas.

It was all enormous fun, but time was running out. At the beginning of April, people began to disappear. Among them was Doreen, to whom Geoff Webb-Bowen had lost his heart months earlier. She was now going home to marry someone else. To my great surprise, as he had never taken the slightest interest in me, he now cast his roving eye in my direction. I knew it was merely boredom on his part, but while it lasted I enjoyed the passionate attention of the most attractive man in Burma.

Just before we both sailed, and after another riotous farewell party – there were many – he made an assignation to meet me at the bottom of the Brownes' garden. I was piqued that he had just picked me up as a plaything, after his own girlfriend had left, and thought I would teach him a lesson. I knew I meant nothing to him. I watched from my bedroom window of the bungalow, as his figure, in creamy dinner jacket, paced up and down in the darkness. After about ten minutes, realising that I was not com-ing, he departed. I felt a certain satisfaction at his discomfiture. (He later told me that his dignity and pride had been 'wounded to the quick'.)

On 15 April Geoff left for England in the *Worcestershire*. He was keen that I should join him, but I could not change my passage from the *Prome*, a fortnight later. With hindsight it was probably for the best, as my resistance would not have held out for a five-week voyage. I did not think I would see him again.

My last day in Burma was 28 April. Six months had flown. My friendship with Margaret, always close, had deepened, and I knew that I would miss her enormously. She was the nearest I had to a sister. It must have been tiresome for Hugh to share his young wife, and occasionally he became possessive. They had both been enormously kind to me and, although I did not know it at the time, had changed the course of my life. They were due to return home in September.

* * *

SS *Prome*, Henderson Line, was a sister ship of the *Salween*. Among the passengers was the senior Royal Air Force officer in the Mis-sion and his family. He arranged that I should sit at the Captain's table with them, which was a big advantage. Also travelling was his wife's niece, who had come out to Burma at about the same time as me. Although she was only twenty-one, she seemed worldly-wise, and I privately thought that she was a hard little piece. One evening, after a few drinks, we had a girlie chat, and she let slip that she had slept with most of the English bachelors. I was shocked – no wonder she looked so sophisticated. When she told me she had had three men in three days, I concluded she must be a 'nympho'. In those pre-pill days, 'nice girls didn't', and no man of husband material, looking for a wife, would have considered a girl who did. I kidded myself that I was saving myself for my husband, but in reality it was the fear of pregnancy that held me back. Girls like Sheila (not her real name) seemed to have no scruples and took great risks.

Merrow Down, Northcroft Road, Englefield Green. My mother built the central part of the house, against stiff opposition from her brother-in-law Stewart, in 1952 for £3,000. The wings were added by subsequent owners. The house is now worth just under £1 million.

After six months away, it was time to settle down. My mother showed me her new creation, Merrow Down, with pride. Despite Stewart's gloomy predictions, she had built a charming small house in Englefield Green which was to be a source of pleasure and income in the coming years. At last our furniture came out of store again, and the drawing-room, which had been designed to take Grandfather McNaughton's bookcase, was an elegant room in a restful shade of eau-de-Nil.

Now, once more, I had to decide what to do with my life. A short time before I left Burma, one of Desmond Parkinson's colleagues in the Embassy asked if I had thought of the Foreign Office as a career and gave me an address to contact. Again, I had a monumental struggle with my conscience, but Margaret and Hugh told me that, at nearly twenty-seven, it was time to look ahead. It did not make the decision any easier. When I told my mother, she was very supportive. On my return home, I was summoned for an interview. Elizabeth Downing, one of the 'Bee's Knees', had also been approached. I saw a large and friendly woman, Frankie Macy, head of Personnel, in an office overlooking Piccadilly. She told me that I would hear from her in about a month, after I had been pv'd (positively vetted), my papers seen by a Board and my references taken up. (I had to provide the names of three people who had known me for five years.) She did not bother with a shorthand test, which pleased me as Elizabeth Downing had had three. Meanwhile, I lived at home and joined Peter Jones' employment agency to fill in time.

One of the most interesting jobs was with some City stockbrokers named Croll. They implored me to forget the Foreign Office and join their permanent staff. I was tempted to do so as I found the work fascinating and learned much about the financial market.

Early that year, in Burma, Jane Downing, the elder of the 'Bee's Knees', had announced her engagement to Jimmy Speirs, a delightful Third Secretary who worked in the same Embassy department as Desmond Parkinson. They were married in Bordon Church, near Hindhead, on 28 June. All the Burma crowd were there and it was the greatest fun. Geoff Webb-Bowen appeared with 'Sheila' on his arm. She looked very proprietorial. To my great surprise, he took me on one side and asked me for a date in London on 14 July. I could hardly believe it. Perhaps the fact that I had refused a passage in *Worcestershire* had made him keener; more likely, it was revenge for his rejection in the garden. Of all the men in Burma, he had been the most aloof. I was determined not to fall in love with him, for I knew that he collected women as a hobby.

On 11 July my mother and I gave a housewarming party at Merrow Down. About fifty people came, mostly my friends from Burma. We started with champagne cocktails and ended dancing reels on the lawn until two in the morning.

Geoffrey had planned my seduction carefully, regardless of expense; to take a girl out today on such a scale would cost the best part of £500. Our date had been postponed by two days as he had been asked to be an usher at the wedding of Gerald Lascelles,[6] a brother officer in the 60th. We met for

To G.H.W-B

Sonnet - Contempt.

Godlike, you sit upon your tinsel throne
Besotted by the clamour of the Crowd;
In that vast multitude, I stand alone,
Unmoved by homage and my head unbowed.
Lo! how they flatter him with roundelays;
See how they love him by their ringing cheers!
Poor blinded fools, he only loves their praise
Whose echo will run lightly down the years.
Go! to those others with their cheaper wares,
Buy them with kisses and your worthless words!
Tell them you love them, that you're wholly theirs,
They will believe you in their sheeplike herds.
Untarnished is my citadel and strong;
Invincible, although the siege was long.

11th to 14th August, 1952

My sonnet 'Contempt', written for Geoffrey Webb-Bowen, 14 August 1952.

95

a drink at the Ritz, and then lunched at Quaglino's. Afterwards we saw *La Ronde*, an amorous French film, at the Curzon cinema. We then changed into evening dress and went off to *Call Me Madam*, an American musical that had taken London by storm. Later, we dined and danced at the Berkeley until 1.30 am. I had asked him to stay the night at home and knew what would follow: a sustained and determined seduction, which fortunately I was strong enough to resist. The next day he was working at the War Office, but he took me off to lunch once more at Quags. Before setting out for Trentham, his Staffordshire home, he drove me back to Englefield Green. In the car going home he said ,'I'm glad you resisted me. You would have regretted it later.' He left at 10.00 pm for his five-hour drive home. He was a practised seducer, but once his quarry had proved inviolable he lost interest. Despite my good intentions, I had fallen deeply in love with him. Never before had I been assailed by such a devastating man. He wrote to me a few times before rejoining his regiment in Germany, but I never saw him again.

On 13 August I heard that I had been accepted by the Foreign Office. I was particularly pleased as others I knew had been turned down. I was to start the following Monday.

Notes

[1] Arterial sclerosis, like my father. In fact, his left lung had been removed.

[2] The country is now Myanmar.

[3] He was a cousin of Elizabeth Colville and also of her mother, Evelyn Webb-Bowen, of Beccles.

[4] Many years later, as Sir William Harding, he served as Ambassador to Brazil from 1981 to 1984 and as Deputy Under Secretary of State at the Foreign Office from 1984 to 1986.

[5] £300 does not seem much in 2010, but over half a century ago it was the equivalent of a year's salary as a secretary.

[6] Brother to the Earl of Harewood and first cousin to The Queen.

Chapter 6

Salvation

'Hide what I have said to thee'

The Two Gentlemen of Verona 4.3.37

There was no reason to think, as I mounted the steps of the red-brick building near St James's Park station, had my new pass checked by security and entered the ancient iron-grilled lift which rose slowly to the fourth floor, that this was one of the many outposts of the Foreign Office in Central London, for it was totally anonymous. There were four new recruits in the room on that hot August day, and we eyed each other warily. The man who now entered was short and stout and had a well-defined military moustache. When he gave his name, I realised that this was none other than the brother of the hero of Alamein.

After a brief preamble, he proceeded to tell us about our future employment. 'You will be working for Sir Patrick Reilly, the Assistant Under Secretary of State. As much of your work will be confidential, you must be circumspect about your job. When you go home tonight, your family will ask you all sorts of questions. Say that you spent the day filling in forms and that sort of thing.'

I did not have to worry about my mother's curiosity. When she met me at Egham station, she asked not a word about my job until a cursory enquiry after supper. I found it easy to blur the outline of my day and, indeed, I never told either of my parents exactly what I did.

The next day I went over to Piccadilly to see Personnel. Here I found Anna, an admiral's daughter and ex-Wren officer who was in charge of foreign postings. (Nearly everyone had naval, military or air force connections – this was how recruiting happened in those days, through the old boys' network.) She asked where I would like to serve. 'Paris,' I replied, knowing it was a very long shot. 'That, I am afraid, is our plum embassy, with a very long waiting list,' she said. 'I shall probably send you to one of our offices in Germany.' I had been warned to resist, as the post-war work there was very boring. I continued to hope that my months in Paris in 1947 and my reasonable knowledge of French might tip the balance.

Several weeks went by. I was happier than I had ever been, and realised that at last I had found the perfect home. Everyone was known by their Christian names, and the work was fascinating. As a new member of staff, I spent the first few weeks getting to know the arcane procedures of the Foreign Service, which had changed little since the days of Palmerston.

One afternoon, Anna recalled me: 'I am pleased to tell you that your posting to Paris has come through. I hope you will be very happy there.' I was elated – it was beyond my dreams.

My mother was very supportive and said she was pleased, although I knew it would be a wrench for her. I admired her resilience, for it cannot have been easy for her to make her own life, living alone without a man. She had a good brain, managed her small financial portfolio and had withstood much opposition from her brother-in-law, Stewart, when building her house. The ubiquitous 'Binks' had departed, and our spare room was now let to a Mrs Lockhart, a worldly, sophisticated bridge player who I hoped would become a good friend.

But before I could go to Paris, there was the coding exam to pass. As I had been a Wren coder, Anna said that I would become a 'codist', as the Foreign Office staff were called. Later, I was amazed to learn that I had passed with 100 per cent. (Trumpet blowing, I know, but I have never divulged this fact before.)

* * *

On Saturday 18 October 1952, I arrived once more at the Gare du Nord. This time there was no Mamzelle Vincent to meet me; instead there was Doreen, one of the senior secretaries, with a large Embassy car. At once, I realised that I had joined a family and would be looked after. All new arrivals were lodged in a small

My lifelong friend Paddy, whom I first met while we were working at the British embassy in Paris, outside our home in Reedham, Norfolk, with our miniature dachshund Oboe, c 1975.

hotel near the Embassy until permanent accommodation could be found.

The next day, after coffee and croissants, Doreen took me to our place of work, a redbrick building off the Faubourg Saint-Honoré, where the overflow Embassy staff were housed. My boss, Alex Mitchell, had not yet arrived, and I spent my time learning the names of the senior diplomats. The head of our section was Victor Bailleau, a tall, bespectacled, serious man of forty-three. In addition there were a dozen or so secretaries, several of whom had unusual linguistic skills. The head secretary, Diana, who worked for Victor, was a grey-haired woman of forty-two who had just returned from Caracas. I shared a large room overlooking the *faubourg* and the British Embassy opposite with Barbara, a vivacious and chatty girl of twenty-three. Her large vocabulary included most of the worst French swearwords (her favourite expletive was *merde!*). She worked for Ben, who liaised with his French counterparts. He was a delightful chap of about forty, sharp as a bird, a fluent French speaker who always wore his OE bow tie.

Next door was Brenda, a handsome woman in her forties who was in charge of admin and pay. Recently divorced, she had a rather forbidding, confrontational manner. I learned that her family came from Norfolk.[1] Her manner appeared to be defensive, but later we became good friends.

Today, the main threat to the western world is thought to come from al Qaeda and militant Islam. In the early 1950s, the enemy was perceived to be Russian. Although the Soviet Union had been our allies in the defeat of Hitler, there was much suspicion of Soviet intentions. In the United States, fear of Communist infiltration of government and the military gave rise to 'McCarthyism', a term coined after the ruthless investigations of the eponymous senator.

In France and other European countries, the same fear ruled. One of our aims in Paris was to combat the Soviet threat. Leading Communists on whom we kept a close eye included Maurice Thorez, the leader of the Communist Party, whose activities were

Memories of France, 1954. Clockwise from top left: Paddy at Blois; Jilly at Tours; a deserted Seine embankment; and Nicolette and Gillian Dold, a Dior model, in Paris (taken by Peter Anson).

constantly monitored. Another was Jacques Duclos, a leading Stalinist.But, apart from work, the most pressing need was to find somewhere to live. I had written to Mlle Vincent, my former tutor, but she could only offer me a shared room in her flat and I wanted some privacy as well as the chance to improve my French. So Doreen took me across the Faubourg Saint-Honoré to the Embassy, a beautiful eighteenth-century house, once the home of Pauline Bonaparte, Napoleon's sister, the Princess Borghese. Here we scanned the list of vacant rooms and apartments approved by the Foreign Office.

The following evening Doreen, who had her own car, drove me round Paris looking for digs. We saw a room in the avenue Wagram, which I didn't think was fit for a dog. There was an ancient iron bedstead and marble busts in the dining-room. The hatchet-faced landlady, who was asking 30,000 francs (about £30) per month demi-pension, looked horrified when I asked whether one could entertain friends in the evening. '*Dans le salon, naturellement, mademoiselle?*' Her relief was palpable when I answered '*mais, bien sûr, madame*'.

After a few days of fruitless searching, I heard from Iona Nimmo, a close friend in England.[2] She put me in touch with a couple in their sixties, undoubtedly members of *le gratin* (the upper crust), with whom she had stayed when doing the Cordon Bleu cookery course some years earlier. Monsieur Guiard, a former Ambassador to Brazil, small and silver-haired, and his tall, rather forbidding wife let their two spare bedrooms in order to eke out a small pension. Their apartment in the rue Spontini was in the *seizième* (the 16th *arrondissement*), an upmarket district inhabited mainly by diplomats and professionals. Nearby was the rue de la Faisanderie where the Gestapo had had their infamous headquarters.

The room Madame Guiard showed me was small and sparsely furnished, but I decided to take it. I would live with them *en famille* and doubtless improve my French. The other, much larger bedroom was let to a handsome young Norwegian, Hans Styrene, who was in Paris for three months on business, leaving his wife in Oslo.

Each morning I walked to Rue de la Pompe metro station or caught the number 63 bus to the Embassy. Each evening I returned for dinner, often a joint of pink *rosbif* served by Catherine, their only maid.

Monsieur Guiard was an historian and his great passion was Napoleon. He loved to recall the battle of Waterloo. Taking up the pepper pot, he announced '*et Napoléon était là.*' Then, seizing the salt cellar, '*et Blücher était là.*' Finally, he took up the mustard: '*et Wellington était là.*' Then would follow a long exposition on the tactics of each General and how Napoleon could have won if only he had done this or that. Madame looked on with a bored expression. She had heard it all before.

The evenings were tedious. After dinner, we repaired to the *salon* for coffee, Monsieur would then take *Le Figaro*, the right-wing daily newspaper, or a book such as Victor Hugo's *Les Misérables*, from which he would read aloud for nearly an hour. At first, I listened intently knowing that it was good for my French, but gradually the exercise palled and I found it difficult to extricate myself. Hans had the good sense to flee to his room immediately after dinner and I wished that I had done the same. My French was still rudimentary and at first I made the mistake, as I rose wearily to depart, of saying, '*Bonsoir, Monsieur et Madame, je vais me coucher,*' which I thought meant that I was retiring to bed. What I had apparently said was '*je vais m'accoucher*' – 'I am going to have a baby.' Madame soon corrected me.

However, Monsieur and Madame did take me under their wing. One evening soon after my arrival, we all went to a *conférence* – a lecture – on Marie Stuart. This was interesting once it got going, but the first hour was spent introducing the dignitaries who bobbed up and down – *Monsieur le Maire, le préfet, le président et al.* French evenings started late, at nine, and we did not get home until nearly midnight.

Early in November, the Guiards took me to High Mass at the church of Saint Eustache, in Les Halles, the huge marketplace where the Feast of St Hubert, the patron saint of hunting, was taking place. The procession of workmen in their medieval shovel hats, looking like cowboys, was followed by huntsmen in pink coats and blowing their horns. The service commemorated the dead of Les Halles who had fallen in both world wars. On 11 November itself, Paris virtually closed down. The few buses running jauntily flew small *tricolores* from their prows like a flotilla of fussy little tugs. A huge flag enveloped the Arc de Triomphe.

Hans Styrene, the handsome Norwegian, was becoming flirtatious. One evening he asked if I would like to go to a *boîte de nuit*, a night club. The philosophy of existentialism, as practised by Jean-Paul Sartre and his mistress, Simone de Beauvoir, had taken hold among the young, and many of their followers congregated in the shady Left Bank haunts of Saint-Germain-des-Prés. And so, the following Saturday, Hans took me to le Vieux Colombier, a dark, noisy, smoky dive where the *chanteuse* was Juliette Greco, not yet the icon she would become. My diary recalls that 'he dances divinely' and that I found him 'most attractive'. Be that as it may, I described the evening as '*très convenable*' (extremely proper), although I rather naughtily wished it hadn't been. Next morning, Madame quizzed me, asking pointedly whether we had gone out in a group or had been alone. I replied truthfully that we were on our own. '*Mais, vous étiez SEULE*'!! she exclaimed, the last word said in the horrified tones of Lady Bracknell's HANDBAG.[3] I thought it was enormous cheek – I was, after all, twenty-seven, and the way I spent my time was none of her business. Had we been speaking in English, I would have told her so, but my French was not yet good enough to stress the point without sounding rude, so I desisted. What I should have said, of course, was '*Honi soit qui mal y pense.*'[4]

It was clear that Madame did not think my behaviour *convenable*, and relations between us grew cooler as the weeks passed. At Christmas, Hans returned to Oslo for good and I asked if I might move into his much larger room. Madame was not pleased. '*La grande chambre est réservée pour un jeune homme,*' she replied. I guessed that she could, of course, charge a young man more. After Christmas, as no suitable *jeune homme* had turned up, she reluctantly agreed that I might move, and, naturally, the rent was increased.

I had, of course, never entered Hans' room, only viewed it from the passage, and once inside was disappointed. Like many French rooms of that ilk, it was dark, with 'morbid striped wallpaper and cherubs cavorting round the ceiling'. I began to grow restive.

* * *

Back in the office, where we still kept leisurely Victorian hours, I was beginning to untangle the mess of unfiled papers and reports left by my predecessor, Christine. The day did not officially start until ten o'clock, which I found much too late, so I often arrived at eight thirty. Conversely, we seldom left till seven.

It was not until 4 November, more than a fortnight after my arrival, that I met my boss, Alex Mitchell. First impressions were mixed – I describe his looks as 'not prepossessing and not at all what I expected – shortish, plumpish and very dark, about forty'. A Welshman, he was an alumnus of Jesus College, Oxford, and very clever. I soon discovered that he was a gem.

Before long I was welcomed into Alex's family and spent much time in their flat high above the Champ de Mars near Les Invalides. Glenys, his pretty wife, was also Welsh, and she and their two children, Katherine and Nicholas, were as warm and friendly as my boss. They treated me like a daughter and I felt very blessed.

Before coming to Paris, several people had given me introductions to friends in the city. One of these was Frances Hobhouse, who had known my stepmother, Nancy, in their university days. She gave me the name of a close friend of hers, who promised to look me up. Max had been expecting my call and asked me to supper on the following night. He and his wife, a flamboyant extrovert called 'Pepi', lived in a flat in the rue Copernic, near the Trocadéro. Max's history was strange and tragic. A Polish landowner and aristocrat, he had been forced to flee with his family when his estate was over-run by the Russians in 1941. Like many refugees, they found their way to Paris where he had been living for the past ten years. Max was a darling man who would sit in his brown corduroy jacket, deep in thought, quietly sucking upon his pipe. His wife was the opposite – a compulsive talker and inclined to histri-onic utterances. Although she called herself 'Pepita' or 'Pepi', she was English and possessed not a drop of Spanish blood. However, she was an inspired cook and I spent many happy evenings with them.

Another friend was a member of a famous literary family – I will call him 'Giles'. He was an incorrigible rake who loved to tell risqué stories. One of his acquaintances was the exiled Queen of a Balkan state whose marriage was in trouble. Still a young and attractive woman, but short of money, she was much sought after. Her price, so 'Giles' told us, was 'a Cadillac a time'. He and a chum, 'GB', hunted as a couple and would often be found relaxing in one of the city's many bordellos. Here they met some voracious 'Madames'. Once, so he told us, he was having problems. From the corner of his eye he saw the Madame bearing down on him, wielding a cane, which she thought would do the trick. 'Giles' disappeared at high speed clutching his trousers.

Other diplomats to whom I had been given introductions were the Press Counsellor, Tom Corley-Smith, and Michael Wilford, then a Third Secretary.[5] Both men were friendly, but once they had done their obligatory duty with a lunch or dinner, one did not hear from them again. An exception was our section head, Victor. He and his wife, Viola, a talented children's author, gathered up any-one alone at Christmas and included them in their festivities. We felt very much part of a family.

On January 10 1953 Jinny married her Anthony in England, and they spent their honeymoon in Morocco. I was delighted to see them when they passed through Paris on their way home, although Jinny had caught a nasty bug from North African food.

At the end of February 1953, Alex's son, eight-year-old Nicholas, contracted septicemia. Although he recovered, the strep-tococci attacked Alex, who became desperately ill. For some time, his life was in danger and it was not until the end of May that he was well enough to return to the office.

* * *

One morning, Geoffrey, who worked for the European Economic Council, dashed into my office in high glee: 'Fantastic news – who do you think is coming to Paris? Nicolette.' I had met her briefly in London three years earlier, but I had no idea what an important part she would later play in my life. Nicolette had joined the Foreign Service through a naval friend of her father's.[6] Pretty, vivacious and intelligent, she quickly made herself at home in Paris, and her flat was always buzzing with young men passing through the city.

Life *chez* Guiard had been becoming steadily more austere since Hans left. Like many Frenchwomen of her ilk, Madame, while outwardly charming, possessed a hard inner kernel of thrift, some would say meanness. She had let my small room to an Australian girl, Fay. Now that she no longer had a man to feed, the standard of food declined. Instead of the *rosbif*, our diet consisted of macaroni and lentils. She was economising. I imagined that she and Monsieur fed on something better for lunch. In addition, there was very little hot water and baths were rationed to one a week. It was time to move on.

Early in March I saw Mrs Errard, who was in charge of accommodation at the Embassy. I wanted to live on my own after the restrictive French and asked her if she had anything on the *rive gauche* – the left bank of the Seine. To my surprise she had.

Rue Servandoni was in the *sixième*, one of the most ancient quarters of Paris. That evening I took the metro to Saint-Germain-des-Prés, crossed the Place Saint-Sulpice with its lovely church (where Marcel Dupré was organist), and entered the narrow medieval Rue Servandoni. This is the historic quarter of Paris where almost every building can tell a story. At number 19, a newer house than some of the others, I took the lift to the top. Here, I was welcomed by Madame Bruller,[7] small, dark and charming. The room, which was prettily furnished with flowered cretonne curtains and bedspread, looked out over the narrow street. The rent was 15,000 francs per month, half what I had been paying *en pension*, and I had the use of the kitchen and bathroom. I took it on the spot.

The Guiards were not pleased. In fact Madame was most un-pleasant. She said I was '*égoiste et éloignée*'[8] – not affectionate like her other *enfants*.

I moved in early in March. It was heaven to be on my own and to be able to entertain my friends. (Needless to say, in true French fashion, the pretty cretonne curtains and bedspread had disappeared, to be replaced by something plainer. When I asked Madame where they were, I was told '*aux nettoyeurs*', at the clean-ers – they never came back. Each evening after work, I caught the metro from Madeleine to Saint-Germain-des-Près. The *rive gauche* had its own magic; even the station names were evocative – La Motte Picquet, Duroc, Sèvres Babylone. Emerging by the cele-brated café Les Deux Magots,[9] near L'Abbaye, the dark and smoky club where Les Frères Jacques performed nightly,[10] I walked the short distance across the Place Saint-Sulpice to a small *charcuterie* and *pâtisserie*. Here I bought *oeufs en gelée* or some other delicacy for my supper, plus a bottle of *vin rouge*. I was very happy.

* * *

On 2 June 1953 Her Majesty Queen Elizabeth was crowned in Westminster Abbey. Despite the heavy rain, three million people lined the streets, many of them having slept out all night. Televi-sion was still a new medium and there had been much discussion as to whether the service should be televised. Both Sir Winston Churchill, the Prime Minister, and the Earl Marshal the Duke of Norfolk, who was in charge of ceremonial, had vetoed the plan, as they felt it would put too much stress upon the young girl who had so recently ascended the throne. The Queen overruled them and insisted that she should be visible to all her people. In the event, the Coronation was watched by some twenty million people, many of whom had never seen television before.

Despite my absence from England, I did not miss this royal oc-casion. Pepi and Max, like many others, hired a television set. They gave a party to which they invited their many friends. We watched the whole occasion live and toasted Her Majesty in delicious Bollinger. The picture, on a small screen, was of course in black and white – colour had not yet reached Europe, and would not become universal for another two decades.

Many of my colleagues in the Embassy had friends passing through Paris who wished to take them out. If they were otherwise engaged, they would ask a chum to take over. One day Doreen asked me if I would entertain a friend of hers who was in the city on business. Most of these chaps were on generous expenses and preferred to spend the evening with someone they vaguely knew than explore the many dives alone or sit by themselves in a lonely hotel room with room service. Stan, a married engineer of about forty, was attentive if unexciting. He took me to the Tour d'Argent, a tourist mecca high above the Seine with amazing views of Notre Dame. It was not in the least French – all the waiters spoke English and the place was full of Americans. We ate caneton Tour d'Argent, the restaurant's speciality, which is extremely rich. The dish consists of two courses. First the duck's breasts are cooked in port and cognac; later the legs are presented in a heavy but delicious sauce. With this we drank Rhône wine and a bottle of champagne. I noted that the meal cost three thousand francs – about £350 today. Stan was determined to savour every moment in Paris, his first visit, so we went on to a nightclub in Montmartre, where we consumed another bottle of champagne. The whole evening had been entirely *convenable* and he had enjoyed himself, which was the object of the exercise. The next day I felt distinctly queasy.

I was gradually getting to know my office companions. There was Anne, small, bespectacled and friendly; Annette, a pretty girl from Jersey who worked for Victor and wore her red hair in a plait round her head and whose Italian boyfriend, Franco, was always hanging about the office; and Rosemary, lively and extrovert. Among the rest was the thirty-three year old 'Paula' (not her real name), tall and stately, whom we nicknamed 'the Duchess'. She had recently acquired a Jewish lover of sixty-two and regaled us with stories of his amazing vigour – 'five times last night' she gasped one morning.

A newcomer to the Embassy at about this time was Paddy, who

worked for the naval attaché. She and I have remained life-long friends.

But the one I remember best is 'Dizzy', then in NATO. At thirty-one, she was already grey, with the air of a wise owl and enormous fun. After a distinguished career in distant lands she became principal of her Oxford college and a governor of the BBC. In 1990 she was created a life peer.

Single men were in short supply. Hugh Jones, the one Embassy bachelor, a lugubrious, unexciting Welshman, was much in demand. One or two of the married men in the office felt it incumbent upon themselves to redress the balance.

About this time, Pepi (who considered herself *in loco matris*) told me it was time I took a lover. Several of the girls in the office had long-term boy friends, but I had not met anyone special and was not sure that I was yet ready to cross this particular Rubicon. Shortly afterwards, I was invited for the weekend by one of the senior diplomats and his wife. (Most of them were extremely friendly and frequently asked us out.) They lived at Malmaison, a pretty *banlieu* about forty-five minutes from Paris. While I was helping him to paint the fence at his home, he told me how wretched his marriage was and asked me to be his mistress. He said we could have 'an arrangement', but that he could not give me, and I was not to expect, 'much affection'. He did not want to have an 'emotional entanglement' and I was not to fall in love with him. Although I found him attractive and was tempted, I found his proposal insulting, and told him so. Pepi, a devout Catholic, agreed with me and told me that it was a mortal sin to have an affair with a married man. He was a close friend of Alex, who, I am sure, guessed what he was up to. Alex was a giant among men, so loyal, so honourable – I would have lost his esteem for ever had I given in. This mindset was typical among some (but not all) of our male colleagues. They seemed to think, in their patronising way, 'You're a single girl – q.e.d. you must be sex-starved – here I am.'

In August, Barbara, my office room-mate, was invalided home with a psychotic illness. She had not been well for some time. She was one of the lucky few who lived in her own apartment. It was a delightful little flat, near the Palais de Chaillot, with its own front door. Some time earlier, she had given me first refusal. I now had to make a snap decision. Most of the good accommodation was handed on by word of mouth – very little went back into the Embassy pool. Although I loved living on the left bank, I decided this was too good an opportunity to miss.

Number 39 avenue Georges Mandel was a smart address. The apartment was on the fourth floor of a handsome *fin de siècle* house. A beady-eyed *concièrge,* who expected monthly gifts of tea, coffee or eggs as a *pourbois* (tip), observed every coming and going. This was the *quartier chic* of Paris, and I was only five minutes away from Pepi and Max. Georges Mandel was a wide tree-lined avenue, down which elegant Frenchwomen, dressed in Dior or Balmain, paraded themselves and their dogs. Sometimes I spotted the famous actor, Jean-Louis Barrault, star of the film *Les Enfants du Paradis,* exercising his large black poodle. Each morning I caught a number 52 bus from Trocadéro.

As soon as I had unlocked my own front door, I felt totally at home. There was a large bed-sittingroom, furnished with elegant Empire furniture, and a small balcony on which one could sit overlooking the courtyard. The bed was covered with a handsome silk bedspread in coffee and cream stripes. Next door was a bathroom, complete with bath, bidet and gas ring, the only cooking appliance. Despite this, I still managed to entertain friends to supper, mainly by using a pressure cooker. From the bathroom, a party door led into the apartment of my landlords, Monsieur et Madame Rouvier. (This was quite a common arrangement in France and was known as a *garçonnière*, a bachelor flat.) The only snag was that the loo was in their flat. One entered immediately into a long hall, which they used as a *salle à manger*. It could be embarrassing, especially if one was entertaining a man, to have to walk the length of their hall while they were dining *en famille* in order to reach the *cabinet de toilette*. '*Bonjour, Monsieur, bonjour Madame.*' '*Bonjour, Mademoiselle, ça va?*' '*Très bien, merci.*' I soon got used to it as there was no alternative. Madame, a handsome middle-aged woman, seemed to spend most of the morning in bed. It was here, each month, that I gave her my rent.

Barbara had warned me that Monsieur was a bit of a wolf. He was a tall, aristocratic looking man in his fifties, and Madame was often away. His favourite ploy was to knock on the communicating door after dinner and ask if one would like to look at his photographs – the French equivalent of 'etchings'. '*Merci, Monsieur, je suis occupée ce soir.*' After several refusals, he gave up.

Alex was now restored to health after his grave illness, and I loved working for him. We were a good team. Much of what we did was absorbing and, one hoped, useful.

By November, the entries in my diary are getting scarce. Nicolette and I had become close friends and she asked me to join a skiing party in Austria over the New Year. Once more, I was in turmoil as I had asked my mother to spend Christmas in my flat. I could not let her down and wrote to say so. Pepi said I should accept – I was now twenty-eight and could not for ever be tied to her apron strings. A few days later, my mother wrote urging me to go. Pepi and Max generously offered to have her to stay. It was a holiday that would change my life for ever.

On Tuesday 15 December 1953, the diary that I had kept for thirteen years, since December 1940, ceased. I had begun to find making the daily entries tedious. It was a pity, as my life was about to enter a new phase and I wish I had a written record. From now on, I have only memory.

Notes

1 Her brother, Philip, a distinguished architect, was knighted in 1980 and served as President of the Royal Academy 1993–99.

2 A dear friend (1925–2009), later married to Michael Bevan, a land agent with Savills now living in north Norfolk.

3 Oscar Wilde, *The Importance of Being Earnest*.

4 'Shame to him who thinks evil.'

5 Appointed as ambassador to Japan in 1975, he received a KCMG in 1976 and GCMG in 1980.

6 Her father was a former naval officer.

7 Shortly after moving in, I checked up on her and discovered that her husband, Jean Bruller, had been a famous fighter in the *maquis* during the war. He was a well known novelist and wrote under the pseudonym 'Vercors'. He was also a Communist sympathiser and was watched by the French authorities.

8 'Selfish and distant'.

9 The haunt of so many famous writers and visitors to Paris: Hemingway, Gide, Sartre, de Beauvoir.

10 A vocal quartet. I can still remember one of their witty and evocative songs: '*N'oubliez pas, Phillibert, ce que t'a dit ta mère, ce que t'a dit ton père, ce que t'a dit ton frère, ce que t'a dit ta soeur – n'oubliez pas Phillibert*': all sung to a rousing and raucous chorus.

Peter Ashley Miller on Dartmoor in 1962, aged thirty-six.

Chapter 7

Anchorage

'Then is all safe, the anchor's in the port'

Titus Andronicus 4.4.38

On Sunday 27 December 1953, Nicolette and I caught the night train for Austria from the Gare de l'Est. We travelled through Switzerland, stopping briefly at Basel. Emerging from the Arlberg tunnel in the early dawn, we woke to a white landscape. The names of the stations – Bregenz, Landeck – took me back three years when I had travelled with my mother to Oberammergau.

At St Anton, we boarded a post-bus up the mountain to Zurs. It was snowing heavily and the bus slithered and slipped over the narrow road. On one side was a steep ravine descending into a turbulent river, and only the driver's skill prevented us toppling over on the hairpin bends. (A friend of Nicolette's had

Our skiing party, January 1955. From left to right: Hugh Sackville West, Judith Maitland, Nicolette, Robin Cotton, and Andrew Chance.

been killed a year earlier when a bus did exactly that.)

Two hours later we found ourselves in Zurs, a tiny Alpine village deep in snow. It was my first visit to the mountains in winter, and the scene was exhilarating. It was nine o'clock and the other four members of our party were still in bed. They were all old friends of Nicolette: Andrew Chance, who lived in Cumberland,[1] Judith Makgill-Crichton-Maitland,[2] Hugh Sackville West[3] and Robin Cotton.[4] They had all come out from London. Apparently Andrew had been horrified when he heard that Nicolette was bringing a friend of twenty-*eight*. 'Good heavens,' he said, 'she must be head of the typing pool.' 'Must be one of Nicky's lame ducks,' said the others.[5] When they had arrived the night before, the manager had taken one look and said, 'Four people – two bedrooms'. Hugh and Andrew obediently shared one, but it took a long time to make it clear that Robin and Judith were not prepared to do the same. Eventually, two single rooms were produced.

Robin and I hit it off immediately and found that we laughed at the same things. After two days, we were putting Christmas trees in each other's beds. On New Year's Eve, we gathered for drinks in my bedroom. Robin suddenly announced that he and Nicolette

Zurs, New Year's Eve 1954. From left to right: Hugh Sackville West, Nicolette, Andrew Chance, Judith Maitland, Jill McNaughton and Robin Cotton. Andrew is wearing Judith's earrings!

had just got engaged to be married. There was a stunned silence. We were all amazed. Then we recovered and charged our glasses.

I learned later that there should have been another member in the party, Peter Ashley Miller, a naval officer stationed at RNAS Stretton in Cheshire. He had fallen foul of his captain, to whom he was secretary. On being instructed to send out invitations to the County for a smart drinks party, he noticed that the invitations had deckled edges – 'GOD not these', he exploded, and refused to send them. He was then put under close arrest.[6]

They were all old skiing friends and had been together four years earlier when George Reindorp, Vicar of St Stephen's, Rochester Row, had taken a party to Murren. This was an annual event for George – he managed to do an exchange with the local padre once a year. Peter had first noticed George at Charing Cross Station: 'what's that fella doing blessing the engine?' The party had also included several pretty nurses from St Thomas' Hospital. Hugh Sackville West had just returned from Nigeria and was in the grip of malaria. Peter's first recollection of Hugh was of the 'blanket bath' gleefully administered by the nurses. They had had a pretty wild time in Murren and one of Peter's favourite stories was of how Judith had had her dress ripped off by a Swiss Guard while dancing a boisterous reel. When Peter was detailed to act as sidesman on Sunday, he was incensed that, while everyone else found Swiss money to put in the plate, Field Marshal Montgomery (Monty), then visiting Murren, produced a button.

We had a hilarious holiday. As I had never skied before, I was put in the beginner's class, joined by Judith and Hugh. (Nicolette had skied in Canada and was rather good.) I soon got the hang of skiing, and improved when I caught the eye of my instructor, Fritz, a handsome Austrian who gave me private lessons free. On the last night, Robin and I decided to play a trick on Andrew.[7] We went to the hotel next door and rang him up. I said that I was 'Daphne Matravers', a friend of a friend (whom we named) ringing from England and that I wished to meet him when he got home in two days time. I gave him the time and place – the Mikado Bar at Claridges. There was much muffled spluttering from Robin in the background which I explained as atmospherics on the line. When we rejoined the party, Andrew told us that an amazing thing had happened, he had been rung up by an unknown girl from England: 'The line was so clear, she could almost have been in the next room.' Whereupon we exploded with laughter and told him that it had been us. The difficult thing was that he absolutely refused to believe us, and was all for dashing off to the Mikado Bar in two days' time. It took some time before we could dissuade him.

Soon we were all back to work. Barbara's replacement in the office was Anne. Small and lively and a fluent linguist, she soon became a good friend, and we went to many concerts and theatres together. I joined a choir, *Les Jeunesses musicales*, and also sang at the Embassy church. When I arrived, the ambassador was Sir Oliver Harvey, who had been appointed by Clement Attlee. (He was known by the writer Nancy Mitford, then living in Paris, as 'utter ghastly drear personified and we all ... say we shan't write our names in *their* book (as if they'd notice).'[8]) The Harveys had had a tough time, having succeeded the legendary Duff and Diana Cooper, who made little effort to ease their passage. Contrary to protocol, the Coopers had remained in France; it was not usual for a retiring ambassador to stay in the country he had served, but the French government had presented them with a *château* in Chantilly in gratitude. The on-going feud between the two couples was well-known. From time to time, Lady Diana, with aristocratic hauteur,[9] would swoop down on the Embassy unannounced and demand objets d'art which she considered were her property and not the British Government's. I sometimes saw her in the NAAFI shop, her beautiful face swathed in a pale blue chiffon scarf.

We, the junior members of the Embassy, were occasionally asked to formal events such as cocktail parties, particularly when the Herveys were replaced in 1954 by Sir Gladwyn and Lady Jebb.[10] [11] I remember one garden party where I spotted a group of people surrounding a man who was treated with a certain amount of deference. As I approached, I recognised the ravaged features, fried-egg eyes and American twang of the erstwhile King of England, now the Duke of Windsor. He and his Duchess, whom I shall always think of as Mrs Simpson,[12] lived in virtual exile in their large house in the Bois de Bologne.[13]

*   *   *

There are many kinds of love – the gentle certainty that someone is so special you cannot live without them (which I had yet to find) – the hot flowering of passion (as I found in Burma) – and occasionally, perhaps once in a lifetime, the *coup de foudre*, a blow so powerful that it almost knocks one sideways. This I was about to discover.

The hub of our social world was Nicolette, whose warmth attracted many friends visiting Paris. Some of them were connections of her naval father who had passed on his charm and gregariousness to his daughter; others were arrivals in the city on business or on holiday.

On Wednesday 26 May, she gave a drinks party. It was the fashion, in those days, to wear hats for these occasions, and I was wearing a most delicious concoction of mother-of-pearl shells, in an 'S' shape, made by a Parisian milliner. (I wish I still had it for it would surely be a museum piece today.) The room was packed. After some time, she brought over a young man of medium height in a brown suit: 'Jill, I don't think you know Peter Anson.' He was in his late

Commander Sir Peter Anson, Bart, Royal Navy, Captain HMS *Broadsword*, 1962, aged thirty-eight.

twenties and I noticed that, although he had a young face, it was unusually ravaged and his hair was iron grey. He told me that he was a Lieutenant Commander in the Navy and was on a NATO course which ended on Sunday. He was not conventionally handsome, but I found him very attractive – he had an animal magnetism that I found hard to resist. After some time, he asked me to go out with him on Saturday. As I was otherwise engaged, I had to decline, whereupon he said that it must be the following night, Thursday.

And so began the most unforgettable few weeks. He came to collect me at Georges Mendel and took me to dine in Montmartre. He had been a seventeen-year-old midshipman in the battleship *Prince of Wales* when she was torpedoed off Malaya in 1941. His captain and 327 of the crew drowned. Anyone who has seen the film *The Cruel Sea* will have a mental picture of hundreds of men swimming in the oily waters desperate to be picked up. Peter and many of his shipmates were captured. Being a Japanese prisoner for four years must have been one of the most horrendous experiences of the war, and it explained his line-drawn face. Thousands died. Those who survived never really recovered and were left with serious psychological scars. He told me that he lived at Hatch Beauchamp in Somerset.[14] [15] Highly intelligent, he was a 'communicator', or a member of the Signals Branch, the elite of the Royal Navy, and was instructing at HMS *Mercury,* the Naval Signal School in Hampshire. After talking far into the night, he took me to l'Eléphant Blanc, the most popular night club in Paris.

As we danced, the chemistry was so intense it almost overwhelmed me – a feeling quite different from Geoffrey Webb-Bowen, because this was mutual.

He said he must see me the following night, Friday, but had to go to an official dinner first. Afterwards, he arrived at Georges Mendel. He crept out in the early hours, hoping not to alert the ever-vigilant *concièrge*.

Nicolette and I spent the weekend away. By this time, being older and wiser and becoming inured to the ways of men, I did not think I would see or hear from him again – despite his apparent feelings.

On Monday evening, I arrived home to find a letter in an unfamiliar hand outside my door. It bore an English stamp and had been posted on Sunday. To my amazement it began 'Little Angel Face'. For the next month, he wrote two or three times a week, each letter more passionate than the last. In one he said he had been to Holy Communion that morning and had 'thanked God for you'. He repeated that he must see me again and asked me to the *Mercury* dance on 2 July. He would book a room in Portsmouth.

On Thursday 1 July I flew to England in a state of high excitement, convinced that I had found my husband at last. Pepi had made me an evening dress in yards of pale pink silk. The dance was heaven. As his partner, I led the eightsome (which luckily I remembered). The next day, we drove into the Hampshire countryside and picnicked in a hidden spot which he obviously knew well. On Sunday, we repeated the experience and on Monday I returned home. Nothing had been said, but the magic had gone. Later I would understand why.

Back in Paris, I wrote to thank him and had a couple of lukewarm letters in reply. I decided I would write no more. I always left for the office early, about seven-thirty, and one morning had an indignant telephone call. 'I rang you last week at eight o'clock – where were you?' I told him I had already left for work. He said he was devastated not to have heard from me for several weeks and, using a 'little boy' voice, begged me to write. I did so but did not hear again. He had had the last word.

* * *

My time in Paris was drawing to a close – my two-year stint ended in October. Alex, too, was departing to a senior post in Cyprus. His friendship, and that of his family, had meant a great deal to me. In August, Glenys gave birth to their third child, a daughter, whom they named Rachel. I was asked to be her godmother. This posed some difficulty as the Mitchells were atheists and at that time I was very religious. George Reindorp advised me to refuse as the title had no spiritual context. I told Alex, who was deeply hurt. I cannot, even now, believe that it was the right decision.

During the summer, Nicolette told me that she and Robin were planning to be married at the end of October. She asked me to be one of her bridesmaids.

I left Paris, with regret, in the middle of the month. Paddy took over my flat and skilfully deflected the amorous advances of Monsieur Rouvier. It had been a period of great happiness – I had made good friends and had had a fascinating job. It was now time to return home. I was going to work for a senior civil servant, a job considered to be something of a plum.

Now I needed somewhere to live. The journey to and from Englefield Green in winter was tiring. Judith Maitland, one of our skiing party, had been offered a flat in Holland Park Gardens, and asked me to share it with her. We had a very happy year together.

Nicolette's wedding was to take place in Suffolk on 30 October. She had arranged for her sister Bridget and Peter Ashley Miller (Robin's best man, now happily released from close arrest) to collect me from my hairdresser at lunchtime the day before. I was intrigued to meet Peter, as Robin had assured me he was rather special. They called, as planned, in George Street, and we walked some way before Peter reminded Bridget that we had not been introduced. I saw a young man of about my own age, of medium height and verging on the plump. He wore specs and was not immediately dishy. He was on leave from Malta and had hired a car to drive up to Pakenham. I had left my case at Marylebone station and was irritated when he did not offer to collect it for me, so I had to get it myself. We had a riotous drive. Bridget sat in the back, munching apples, and Peter and I shared a flask of brandy (which Bridget refused). He told outrageous stories and I began to think that, despite his unprepossessing looks, he was rather fun.

We got to Pakenham at teatime, where the rest of the wedding party had gathered. Nicolette's mother (whom I thought quite old, though she was probably in her early fifties) was a tall good-looking woman of great charm, like her daughter. She was one of those people whom one described as 'a pillar of the community' – after a married lifetime in the Navy, she and her husband had returned to the family home, where she ran the Mother's Union and the

The marriage of Robin and Nicolette, Pakenham, Suffolk, October 1954. From left to right: Alison Cecil; Peter Ashley Miller (best man); Barbara (bride's sister); the groom and bride; Bridget (bride's sister); Jill McNaughton.

Nicolette's bridesmaids, October 1954: Alison Cecil, Jill McNaughton, Bridget and Barbara, the bride's sisters.

After the wedding: Jilly leading, followed closely by the best man, Bridget (the bride's sister) and the four parents.

After the wedding: Jilly leading, followed closely by the best man, Bridget (the bride's sister) and the four parents.

Women's Institute and was a strength and solace to all, as her daughter is today.

The other bridesmaid, apart from Nicolette's sisters, Bridget and Barbara, was Alison Cecil, whom I had met in Paris. She was Peter Anson's cousin. After a family dinner party, we played charades. I was in Peter Ashley Miller's team, and our word was Bury St Edmunds. I was chosen to be the saint, and was wrapped in a sheet and carried into the drawing-room amid great hilarity. As I was being lifted into my coffin, I felt fingers tickling my ankles, and had no doubt to whom they belonged.

The wedding in the ancient church was beautiful – the union of two people who loved each other very much and who have gone on to enjoy a long and fruitful marriage. At the reception Peter was very flirtatious. When I was cagey about where I worked, he said, 'Oh, I suppose you're one of the Curzon Street girls.' Not a bad guess, but they were MI5. Peter himself was in Naval Intelligence, though I did not know it at the time. He asked me if I would go skiing with him in the spring. I was surprised at such a fast worker, and, although still raw and bruised from Anson, enjoyed the attention. He did not stay long but dashed off to Cambridge (where he was meeting a girl)[16] before returning to Malta. A few days later, I got home from work to find a letter with a Maltese stamp, and we began a stately correspondence.

In November, I picked up *The Times.* Heading the engagement column was 'Lieutenant Commander Sir Peter Anson, Bart., R.N. to Miss Elizabeth Clarke'. Nicolette rang me at the office and asked whether he had told me beforehand. When I replied 'no', she said, in a furious voice, 'How *damnable*'. It is the only time I have heard Nicolette swear. Peter Anson was a career naval officer, and an admiral's daughter was a much better catch than me. Clearly he had decided to marry her before our *Mercury* weekend, which explained his coolness. In reply to my letter of congratulation, he told me that she was a barrister and that they were marrying in January. I was deeply hurt, for I had fallen very much in love. I did not recover for some months.[17]

* * *

The first few months of 1955 were not happy. I disliked my new boss, a most unpleasant man, who was a bully. I will call him 'Ernest'.

'Ernest' was very small – five foot three or four – and to compensate threw his weight around. He had been one of the youngest Brigadiers in the war at twenty-six, had thin sadistic lips and a tongue like a viper He also had a dirty mind and was fond of annotating the signal file which did a daily round of the office. One comment, describing a difficult operation by a female diplomat read: 'Penetration was achieved.' In the margin, my boss had pencilled 'lucky girl'. How very different from Alex.

After enduring his bullying and ill temper for some time, I went to see Anna, now Head of Personnel, and asked for a change. A short time later I heard that 'Ernest' was to be posted to Cairo and that I had a new boss. Ned was a delightful young man who had recently returned from Prague and a welcome change from 'Ernest'.[18]

The letters from Malta were becoming more frequent, and more flirtatious. We arranged to ski with a party from Ingham's

Peter and Jilly at Hochsölden, Austria, in April 1955 before their engagement.

(the ski travel specialists), who were going to Hochsölden in Austria. Nicolette's mother, when she heard that Peter and I were going alone, was very shocked, rather like Madame Guiard's reaction when I went out with the handsome Norwegian in Paris. The fact that there were twenty-eight other people in the party did not seem to make much difference.

We were going late, at the end of March, as this was the only time Peter could get leave. I caught the train from Victoria, with the rest of the Ingham's party, and once more travelled through France and Switzerland to the Arlberg tunnel. We got out at Landeck this time, and caught a bus. There was not much snow on the lower slopes, but the scene changed as soon as I got into the chairlift for the steep rise to Hochsölden, which at 6,000 feet is one of the highest Alpine villages. I swung through a silent white world as the chairs travelled slowly upwards through the pine forest. It was magical and I felt deeply at peace, as if I knew that the most momentous time in my life was about to arrive.

* * *

Peter was waiting at the hotel, having arrived by air from Malta. Almost at once, we were at ease with each other and I realised he was someone very special. He had a wicked sense of humour and made me laugh.[19] At last, at the age of twenty-nine, I had grown up. All my life, until then, I had fallen for good-looking, handsome men. At long last, I had learned to look beneath the surface. He was not an Adonis – nor was he a man of straw. He was sensitive about his looks and always said, 'You can't fall for me – I'm just a

126

little fat man in glasses.' But inside was someone whose strength and integrity were unfailing – he was pure gold.

Jilly with her hickory skis, taken by Peter.

When, towards the end of the fortnight, he asked me to marry him, I did not falter. This man contained an inner core of steel that would never shatter. I had found my lynchpin.

After telling my mother, we decided to keep our engagement unofficial until he came home from Malta in October. All through the summer, he wrote me letters of great tenderness nearly every day. I turned to poetry, my unfailing muse, to express my feelings (see page 128).

On 15 October, he came home. We met in the bar of the Berkeley – I wore a grey coat and skirt with a pink feathered toque. It was an emotional meeting. Some days later, he took me to meet his parents, who lived in Pembroke Square. I felt at home at once. I also met his brother Michael, who had just qualified as a doctor.

Coming home: taken by Peter in the Austrian train after we had become engaged.

To P.A.M.

Heart of my inmost heart,
Soul of my soul.
Thine the Creator's art,
Making me whole.

Safe in thy guardian arms
Quietly I lie;
Protected from all alarms,
At peace am I.

Lamp of my unlit night
Star of my sky;
Be thou my guiding light
Until I die.

Brother and lord in one,
Lover and friend.
Be near me when day is done,
World without end.

cjm 8.vii.55.

Marjorie and Cyril Ashley Miller, my parents-in-law, to whom I was devoted.

The whole family had the same delicious sense of humour.

At the end of the month, I took him down to Englefield Green, to meet my mother. Although she had previously said she was delighted, when it came to the crunch she did not want to let me go. I suppose it was understandable. She had had me for nearly thirty years. Her first words to Peter, when they were alone, were 'I hope your intentions are honourable.' She had chosen the wrong man to insult.

My mother had been planning a visit to her sister Evelyn in Australia in February, and felt that this precluded her giving a reception. This saddened me, as I was her only daughter and I felt she might have postponed her departure. Peter, too, was disappointed. In May he would start a course at Greenwich, where he hoped to be married in the Royal Naval Chapel with a Guard of Honour and all our friends, but I felt we could not do so with an absent mother. So we had to settle for a slimmed-down wedding before she left. My mother, busy with travel arrangements, took little part. Peter's parents nobly stepped in and offered Pembroke Square. As their drawing-room was not enormous, we were limited to fifty guests. When I started making the list, my mother said, 'We *must* have The Family.' And so it was that most of the guests were the Kitson aunts and their spouses, thus excluding my close friends. Fortunately, Hugh and Margaret were able to be there. Neither Jinny nor Nicolette could come, as they were dealing with babies, but Robin and Michael were ushers.

We were married by George Reindorp at St Stephen's, Rochester Row on Saturday 11 February 1956, one of the coldest days of the year. My father gave me away. As we were early, we drove several times round Parliament Square, saying little to each other. It was the last time we were alone together in my single state but there was no final *tendresse*. In fairness, I don't think he was well. He continued to have breathing problems stemming from war injuries but exacerbated by heavy smoking. In the photographs on pages 132 and 133 he seems to be clutching his side in pain. Judith Maitland was my bridesmaid in a lovely dress of scarlet brocade. The best man, David Robertson-Macdonald, was Peter's oldest friend – they had met in their prams. The pre-wedding disappointments failed to mar the day. I knew that I was the luckiest and happiest girl in the world. This man was no pusillanimous weakling, but someone whose strength would uphold me in the challenging days that lay ahead.

Left to right: Peter Ashley Miller, aged nine, the future head boy of 'Gladstone's' (Eaton House Preparatory School); as a thirteen-year-old Dartmouth cadet in September 1939; and as House cadet captain of Grenville, at the Royal Naval College Dartmouth *c* 1943.

Notes

1 His father was Lord Lieutenant.
2 She was George Reindorp's secretary at St Stephen's, Rochester Row.
3 Then in the Colonial Service in Nigeria. His family lived at Knole. In 1957, he married Nicolette's sister Bridget.
4 After war service in India as a Sapper he joined Metal Box.
5 All have remained lifelong friends.
6 Peter had known Nicolette when he was a Dartmouth cadet. He had also known Robin's family in Liverpool during the war.
7 An 'other ranker' in the Scots Guards, he had refused to take the commission offered just before D-Day as he did not want to desert his friends. As a result, he had been severely wounded by a shrapnel wound in the head in the push for Falaise.
8 *The Letters of Nancy Mitford and Evelyn Waugh*, edited by Charlotte Mosley, Hodder and Stoughton, 1984, page 84.
9 It was common knowledge that 'Lady Diana' had been born out of wedlock. Her father was apparently not the Duke of Rutland, but Harry Cust, a handsome lothario.
10 As Cynthia Gladwyn, she has written two fascinating books: *The Paris Embassy* (Collins, 1976), a biography of the house and a waspish, gossipy journal, *The Diaries of Cynthia Gladwyn* (edited by Miles Jebb, Constable, 1995).
11 The Jebbs were succeeded in 1965 by Sir Patrick and Lady Reilly.
12 Now owned by Mohamed Fayed and bought by him in the hope that it would become the Paris home of his son, Dodi, and Diana, Princess of Wales.
13 At the time of the abdication in December 1936, we sang, 'Hark the herald angels sing, Mrs Simpson's pinched our King.'
14 His father, Sir Edward Anson, who was descended from a distinguished naval family, had died in 1951, and he was now the 7th baronet.
15 As a Dartmouth cadet, he was a year senior to my husband.
16 The Lady Olivia Taylour, a long-term mistress.
17 Peter retired as a Rear Admiral CB, and then became Chairman of Marconi Space Systems Ltd and later High Sheriff of Surrey. His wife was Chairman of the Association of District Councils from 1991 to 1993 and was appointed DBE in 1994.
18 Ned proposed my health at my leaving party in January 1956. His son, Frank, is the BBC's security correspondent, seriously injured in Saudi Arabia in 2004.
19 Many of the letters I had after he died recalled his 'outrageous' wit.

Clockwise: invitation to the wedding of Peter Ashley Miller and Jill McNaughton, 11 February 1956; the bride and her father; the best man, Lieutenant Commander David Robertson-Macdonald, Peter and Jilly, and Judith Makgill-Crichton-Maitland, bridesmaid.

Clockwise: the ushers, Robin Cotton and Dr Michael Ashley Miller, looking chilly; four guests, Hugh and Margaret Browne (my double cousin) and Enid and Stewart Mc-Naughton (my aunt and uncle); my bridesmaid, Judith Makgill-Crichton-Maitland, and my mother outside St Stephen's; my father, looking frail, my mother, and Peter's parents; and Judith, my bridesmaid.

Mrs Peter Ashley Miller, May 1956, a studio portrait by Elliott and Fry. My mother refused to accept this photograph as a present, saying 'You look so hard.' I had simply grown up.

Envoi

After a ski-ing honeymoon in St Anton, Peter and I moved into our rented flat at 87 Lansdowne Road, Holland Park. It was small. We had one bedroom, a sitting-room, kitchen and bathroom for which we paid our French landlady six and a half guineas a week.

Peter was working in Naval Intelligence at the Admiralty, where his boss was the brilliant Peter White who had come to my twenty-first dance as Audrey Wallin's partner (whom he married).[1] Three months later, my husband started his course at the Royal Naval College and drove to Greenwich each day in our new car, a second-hand baby Austin which we christened 'the little worm'.

Our first home, the top flat at 87 Lansdowne Road, W11.

The news, in July, that President Nasser of Egypt had nationalised the Suez Canal put all military forces on alert. Peter was sent to Malta to prepare for a possible invasion by Britain and France. Tension was high. He returned after several weeks, but soon became seriously ill. Paratyphoid was diagnosed and he was rushed to the Naval Hospital at Chatham. On his recovery, in September, he learned that he was to join HMS *Cumberland*, then lying in Plymouth harbour.

In October, I drove down to Devon alone in 'the little worm' and started to search for accommodation. Tension in the Middle East had reached boiling point. A few weeks later, on 29 October, Israel invaded Egypt and the short Suez Canal war began. The reputation of Sir Anthony Eden, the Prime Minister, was irrevocably tarnished when he denied in the House of Commons that there had been collusion between Britain and France, who supported Israel in an effort to regain possession of the Canal. Most people knew that this was untrue.

From a Plymouth guest house, I spent the next few weeks searching for somewhere to live. Eventually, we moved into Prince Arthur House in a small village, Mary Tavy, just north of Tavistock and on the edge of Dartmoor.

We had been hoping to start a family and in March 1957 I was delighted to find I was pregnant. On 6 December I gave birth in Freedom Fields hospital to a beautiful daughter whom we named Bridget. The following autumn I became pregnant again, but miscarried in October when staying with my cousin Margaret. Peter was told by the doctor to throw the twelve-week-old foetus into the boiler, and was distressed to find that it was male.

The following year, 1959, our love for each other would be tested in a way that would have been unimaginable when we married.

In July, and six months into my third pregnancy, my membranes ruptured. I was rushed into Plymouth hospital where I lay supine until 6 October.[2] There was clearly something grievously wrong when I saw my second daughter, and I guessed at once the condition from which she suffered. From her mouth protruded a large, red tongue and her face was squashed and ugly. Later that day we learned she was what was then called a 'mongol'. Thankfully this pejorative term has been replaced by the gentler 'Down's Syndrome'. We were told that parents were seldom informed until much later and that we were 'victims of our own intelligence'.

Few marriages survive without difficulties. If the union is weak, something will break. If it is strong, the bonds will be strengthened and endure until death. Fortunately I had married a man whose strength would hold me together when I could so easily have cracked. I found myself unable to love this ugly little creature for fifteen years, but she and her father forged a bond that endured until his death. When she was not yet four, and this is something I deeply regret, our doctor advised us to send her away 'for the sake of her siblings'. (In 1962 the birth of Mark had given us great joy.) This was the current thinking. We found a convent where saintly Benedictine nuns looked after her until she was fifteen, when she came home for good. It was only then that I realised what a treasure I had been given.

It was about this time that Peter decided to leave the Navy. There were several options for his future life, and he was asked to be the Tory candidate for Tavistock (later held by Michael Heseltine). He decided instead to take articles with a local firm of chartered accountants and he qualified four years later. By this time we had bought Netherton House, in the village of Buckland Monachorum, ten miles north of Plymouth – our first real home and one which I loved. The political pull was great but the lure of the big city was greater. In 1965 we left our beautiful house and moved near Sevenoaks from where Peter commuted to London each day. He joined the stockbrokers, Hoare, Govett, and was later invited on to the Court of the Ionian Bank. He was now a merchant banker.

The children were growing up. Bridget had joined Cobham Hall as a day girl and later as a boarder. Catherine was still at her convent near Aylesbury, and I drove the six-hour round trip every six

Netherton House, Buckland Monachorum, Devon, the first house we owned. We lived there from 1960 to 1964.

weeks to bring her home. In 1971, when Mark was only eight, he went to board at Sandroyd in Wiltshire, where the two sons of close Devon friends were also educated. This was the ethos of the day, but I shall always regret missing those years with my son.

Peter had always loved Norfolk, where he had spent childhood holidays, and in the summer of 1971 we bought Reedham Old Hall opposite the ancient church in a small marshland village. From its station Peter left home at six o'clock every Monday morning, returning on Friday evening. He loved the house and its surroundings, but I felt isolated in a place where I had few friends. By this time Bridget had left Cobham, which she hated, and travelled by train each day to Norwich High School which gave her an excellent education.

In 1974 the convent that cared for Catherine closed due to lack of nuns and she came to live at home. Later she joined Burlingham House, a residential home only ten miles away, where she lived very happily for thirty years until it closed, through lack of funds, in 2008.

Peter Ashley Miller, head of Private Clients at Arbuthnot Latham, *c* 1981.

Peter's reputation in the City was increasing, and in 1980 he was invited to join the old established merchant bank of Arbuthnot Latham, where he became head of private clients.

In 1981 Reedham parish church burned down, and, as Peter was now churchwarden, he was in his element directing the rebuilding which, under his leadership, was achieved in just over a year. But the years of constant travel

Our three children on holiday at Cley, Norfolk, 1969: Bridget (eleven); Mark (six), holding George, our cat; and Catherine (nine).

and the stress of city life took their toll, and in 1986 he was admitted to Papworth hospital for a quadruple heart bypass. His health deteriorated, and in 1988 he decided to sell our Norfolk home and move to a small house in a Suffolk market town. It broke his heart to do so, for he was a countryman and hated the nine years he lived in Beccles. While he bought a boat and spent much time sailing on the Waveney, I found mental stimulus in the Open University, taking three degree courses in Shakespeare, history and Latin. In 1994, to our great joy, Mark married Fiona Knocker, and two years later their daughter, Catriona, was born. Bridget meanwhile had gained an MA in Contemporary Art and after owning her own gallery became a successful art adviser in London.

And what of the wider family? My father and Nancy moved from London to a Wiltshire cottage in 1954 where his gas-related emphysema eventually caught up with him; he died there in 1959. Nancy proved to be a most generous step grandmother and often came to stay with us in her widowhood.

Peter's father died in 1963 having met his only grandson, Mark, now a year old. His mother, to whom I was deeply attached, died in 1975 having spent her last years happily ensconced in the upmarket retirement home of Hedingham Castle, Essex.

After my marriage, my own mother sold her Englefield Green house at a handsome profit. Although she came to stay with us often, she became increasingly lonely, spending her time in hotels where she was able to play bridge all day and every day. Gradually life ceased to have any meaning for her. She joined the organisation

My seventieth birthday at Bally-gate, Beccles.

then known as 'Exit'. Early in September 1976 she entered a Bournemouth nursing home owned by a doctor who specialised in helping people who were tired of life in this world to enter the next. She died there on 6 September, ostensibly of a heart attack, aged eighty-two.

Peter Ashley Miller, taken by Bridget three months before he died.

As I have said, Peter hated his life in Beccles, and sadly did not live to see the birth of his grandson, William, in 1998 nor the joy that Bridget would find in her friendship with Nick Leon. Catherine, too, leads an independent life in a Norwich bungalow, lovingly cared for by Mencap.

In April 1997 I was diagnosed with breast cancer, a gene that runs strongly on both sides of my family, and underwent a radical mastectomy. Although I received the news calmly, it was something Peter had always dreaded and undoubtedly hastened his death.

On Monday 15 September 1997 I bade him farewell at Beccles station as he left for a board meeting of the bank in London (he remained a non-executive director). I assured him that I would meet his train next day.

At five o'clock that evening, the front door bell rang. Outside stood two policewomen. 'I'm afraid it's bad news. Your husband collapsed on the escalator at Green Park station at ten past three and died later in St Thomas' Hospital.'

It was the end of an era. Now, as I look forward to my new life in Sherborne, near to my family and beloved grandchildren, I thank God for His many blessings.

Mutatis mutandis[3]

Notes

[1] See page 21 and *Not the Purser's Daughter?*, note 21, page 137.

[2] I have written at length about this traumatic time in three articles: *The Times*, 11 October 1971; *The Times*, 8 August 2000; *The Lady*, 17 November 2009.

[3] The necessary changes having been made.

Mourning Song',
written at Beccles,
7 April 1998, seven
months after Peter
died.

Mourning Song

I did not know how death would come

* * *

I always thought the cross's power
Would shield me from the evil hour
When I should stand alone.
Not the shrill telephone
But other bell, on the insistent street
Proclaimed my knell.

* * *

Two females stand, in navy blue,
With whistles, mobile phones,
To tell me you,
The light and laughter of my life,
Have gone.

142

Beccles, 7th April 1998

IN MEMORIAM

Peter Dallas Ross 1921–2010

I had thought that this memoir would end with my husband's death, but fate intervened. To fall in love, four years later, at the age of seventy-six, to fall so deeply in love, to be again so vibrantly alive, was beyond imagining.

Without the electronic wizardry of the twenty-first century, it might never have happened. I don't know what made me send a card to my very first love, Peter Dallas Ross, for his eightieth birthday on 19 November 2001, but in so doing I changed my life. Although I had refused his proposal of marriage fifty-four years earlier, I had never forgotten him – nor he me. After his wedding in 1949 we lost touch. There were one or two Christmas cards, a few sightings from mutual friends, then silence. Much later, I heard that, after twenty four years of marriage and five children, there had been a divorce. So when his card slipped from my fingers into the open mouth of the Beccles postbox on 16 November, and I thought 'what on earth am I doing?', it was with little hope of a response. I had found his name in a medical directory at the library, but there was no way of knowing whether he was alive, dead or merely gaga. I noted, with interest, that he had an email address. Within two hours of receiving my card, he sent an ecstatic reply, and so our love affair, dormant but never dead, was rekindled after nearly sixty years. The spark, smouldering, had never gone out.

Almost at once, we began to email every day. He told me that, after fifteen years of loneliness, he had remarried, not entirely successfully. Our letters, tentative and wary at first, became warmer and less restrained. The formal minuet, as we circled round each other, and which each knew the other was performing, lasted less than three weeks. Shortly before Christmas, we both realised that we had fallen in love all over again.

For five months, until April, our daily epistolary courtship continued.

Our feelings were now so strong that we had to meet. But before doing so, we agreed we would not telephone, lest we should lose the magic. Once more, fate intervened. His computer crashed and we had a weekend in which we lost all contact. On the Monday evening, late, after ten o'clock, a time I have told the children never to ring, unless for a dire emergency, the telephone shrilled. An unfamiliar, deep male voice asked for 'Jilly'. After fifty-four years, I did not recognise him and he had to say, in a tone of exultation – 'Peter'. The pain of three days' separation had been so great that he had *had* to ring. We arranged that I should drive up to Scotland and meet him in a Perthshire hotel – Ballathie.

Friends, and my children, feared the reunion would not be a success – that, having built up to this height of emotion, we would not be able to sustain it. Perhaps, like my mother and her Canadian lover, meeting after two decades, there would be nothing to say. It was not so.

When the telephone rang in my hotel bedroom, to tell me he was downstairs, I waited, in trepidation. Almost at once, there was

To P.D.R.': written on 25 April 2002, the day of our reunion at Ballathie after fifty-three years.

To P. D. R.

Ballathie, Ballathie, sweet sister of Crathie,
Within sound of the fast-flowing stream,
It was here, by the Tay, on an April day,
That my lover came home to me.
Thorough pain, thorough mire,
Thorough loss, thorough fire,
My lover came home to me.
And the years rolled away
As we lingered that day,
By the banks of the sparkling Tay.

Ballathie,
25 April 2002

Family group for my eightieth birthday at the Farmers' Club, SW1, September 2005. From left to right: Peter Dallas Ross, Catriona, Mark, Jilly, William, Bridget, Catherine and Fiona.

a quick knock on the door, and before waiting for an answer he bounded in, bearing flowers and a bottle of Lynch Bages, and enfolded me in his arms.

Dining alone at Ballathie that night, the years rolled away. We were again our younger selves on the evening he had proposed in 1947. Holding hands, and absorbed in each other, we failed to notice that the dining room was empty.

Years ago, I thought I loved him, but I did not love him enough, which is why I refused his offer of marriage. We hardly knew each other. There was no instant communication, no texting, no mobiles. Now, today, in my seventy-seventh year, I know what it is to love him in body, mind and spirit.

Where do we go from here? There is no question of divorce. We are not here to hurt others. Instead, we treasure every moment we can be together, savouring the renewal of a love which we thought had gone for ever.

If my children sense disloyalty to their father, they need not fear. He would delight in my happiness. I never thought it would be possible to love a second time, but so it is. I echo George Herbert's words: 'And now, in age, I bud again.'

It is a miracle.

This was written in June 2002, two months after our reunion. We had over eight wonderful years meeting when possible but otherwise communicating by voice and email. Peter died in Perth, after a short illness, aged eighty-eight, on 13 March 2010.

Requiescat in pace

Index

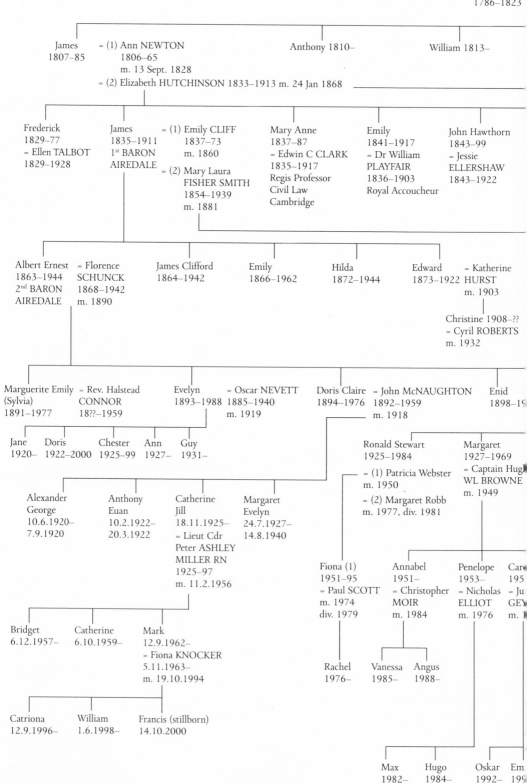

William Kits•
1786–1823

James = (1) Ann NEWTON   Anthony 1810–   William 1813–
1807–85   1806–65
           m. 13 Sept. 1828
         = (2) Elizabeth HUTCHINSON 1833–1913 m. 24 Jan 1868

Frederick   James   = (1) Emily CLIFF   Mary Anne   Emily   John Hawthorn
1829–77   1835–1911   1837–73   1837–87   1841–1917   1843–99
= Ellen TALBOT 1st BARON   m. 1860   = Edwin C CLARK = Dr William   = Jessie
1829–1928   AIREDALE   1835–1917   PLAYFAIR   ELLERSHAW
                           = (2) Mary Laura   Regis Professor 1836–1903   1843–1922
                                FISHER SMITH   Civil Law   Royal Accoucheur
                                1854–1939   Cambridge
                                m. 1881

Albert Ernest = Florence   James Clifford   Emily   Hilda   Edward   = Katherine
1863–1944   SCHUNCK   1864–1942   1866–1962   1872–1944   1873–1922   HURST
2nd BARON   1868–1942   m. 1903
AIREDALE   m. 1890
                                                                      Christine 1908–??
                                                                      = Cyril ROBERTS
                                                                      m. 1932

Marguerite Emily = Rev. Halstead   Evelyn   = Oscar NEVETT   Doris Claire = John McNAUGHTON   Enid
(Sylvia)   CONNOR   1893–1988   1885–1940   1894–1976   1892–1959   1898–19
1891–1977   18??–1959   m. 1919   m. 1918

Jane   Doris   Chester   Ann   Guy   Ronald Stewart   Margaret
1920–   1922–2000 1925–99   1927– 1931–   1925–1984   1927–1969
                                                                = (1) Patricia Webster = Captain Hug•
                                                                m. 1950   WL BROWNE
Alexander   Anthony   Catherine   Margaret   = (2) Margaret Robb m. 1949
George   Euan   Jill   Evelyn   m. 1977, div. 1981
10.6.1920–   10.2.1922– 18.11.1925– 24.7.1927–
7.9.1920   20.3.1922   = Lieut Cdr 14.8.1940
                            Peter ASHLEY
                            MILLER RN   Fiona (1)   Annabel   Penelope   Car•
                            1925–97   1951–95   1951–   1953–   195•
                            m. 11.2.1956   = Paul SCOTT = Christopher = Nicholas   = Ju
Bridget   Catherine   Mark   m. 1974   MOIR   ELLIOT   GE•
6.12.1957–   6.10.1959–   12.9.1962–   div. 1979   m. 1984   m. 1976   m. 1
                           = Fiona KNOCKER
                           5.11.1963–
                           m. 19.10.1994   Rachel   Vanessa Angus
                                                                            1976–   1985–   1988–
Catriona   William   Francis (stillborn)
12.9.1996–   1.6.1998–   14.10.2000

                                                               Max   Hugo   Oskar   Em
                                                               1982–   1984–   1992–   199•